PEARSON

ALWA D0087854

Lorraine D. Cross • Barbara Pullease • Hope Waldman Targoff

Demonstrating the New Florida Educator Accomplished Practices

A Practical Guide for Becoming an Effective Educator

Pearson Learning Solutions, 501 Boylston Street, Suite 900, Boston, MA 02116
A Pearson Education Company
www.pearsoned.com

Printed in the United States of America

1 2 3 4 5 6 7 8 9 10 V363 16 15 14 13 12 11

000200010270648399

MT

ISBN 10: 1-256-05197-7
ISBN 13: 978-1-256-05197-8

PREFACE

The Florida Educator Accomplished Practices (FEAPs), adopted by Florida's State Board of Education in July 1998, were created to (1) identify state standards for effective instructional practice and (2) define and identify effective teaching practices. Revised and approved in December 2010, the FEAPs presently "form the foundation for the state's teacher preparation programs, educator certification requirements, and school district instructional personnel appraisal systems" (Florida Department of Education, State Board Rule 6A-5.065, p. 1).

<u>**This book is intended to be a resource and guide for individuals:**</u>
- new to the education profession,
- seeking Alternative Certification,
- seeking to pass the Teacher Certification Exam or Professional Education Exam, and
- seeking Education Certification.

<u>**The book is also intended as a resource and guide for:**</u>
- coaches and mentors of new teachers,
- experienced teachers,
- school administrators, and
- participants in state-approved Alternative Certification programs.

<u>**This book contains the following features:**</u>
- research and resources on effective teaching practices, and
- activities that give the user the opportunity to demonstrate and reflect on the indicators of the Florida Educator Accomplished Practices.

<u>**This book is organized by the Florida Educator Accomplished Practice. Each Educator Accomplished Practice is divided into the following sections**</u>:

- ***DID YOU KNOW*** – This section includes an introduction to the Florida Educator Accomplished Practice (FEAP) and vocabulary associated with the FEAP.

- ***WHY WE KNOW*** – This section includes a summary of research related to the Florida Educator Accomplished Practice.

- ***WHAT YOU NEED TO KNOW*** – This section includes a summary of best practices related to the Florida Educator Accomplished Practice.

- ***LET IT SHOW*** – This section includes a list of teacher products and activities that demonstrate teacher competency of the Florida Educator Accomplished Practices indicators.

TABLE OF CONTENTS

UNIT 1: QUALITY OF INSTRUCTION

Chapter 1: INSTRUCTIONAL DESIGN AND LESSON PLANNING

Chapter 2: THE LEARNING ENVIRONMENT

Chapter 3: INSTRUCTIONAL DELIVERY AND FACILITATION

Chapter 4: ASSESSMENT

Chapter 6: PROFESSIONAL RESPONSIBILITY AND ETHICAL CONDUCT

QUALITY OF INSTRUCTION

FLORIDA EDUCATOR ACCOMPLISHED PRACTICES

- **#1: Instructional Design and Lesson Planning**
- **#2: The Learning Environment**
- **#3: Instructional Delivery and Facilitation**
- **#4: Assessment**

INSTRUCTIONAL DESIGN AND LESSON PLANNING

Applying concepts from human development and learning theories, the effective educator consistently:

- **Aligns instruction with state-adopted standards at the appropriate level of rigor**
- **Sequences lessons and concepts to ensure coherence and required prior knowledge**
- **Designs instruction for students to achieve mastery**
- **Selects appropriate formative assessments to monitor learning**
- **Uses a variety of data, independently, and in collaboration with colleagues, to evaluate learning outcomes, adjust planning and continuously improve the effectiveness of the lessons**
- **Develops learning experiences that require students to demonstrate a variety of applicable skills and competencies**

Florida Educator Accomplished Practice #1:

INSTRUCTIONAL DESIGN AND LESSON PLANNING

DID YOU KNOW…

Introduction:
Teachers align their lessons with state standards, of course; but they also plan the activities to go with their lesson's objectives, the materials they will use, how they will differentiate their lessons for their diverse learners, and how they will engage their students and assess their progress. Effective teaching requires knowledge, dedication, and a lot of planning!   Good planning results in a smooth running classroom with few behavior disruptions.

Vocabulary:

behavioral objective – a statement of expectation describing what the learner should be able to do upon completion of the instruction, and containing four components: the audience (learner), the overt behavior, the conditions, and the level or degree of performance; also referred to as performance and terminal objective

choral reading – a reading strategy that helps students focus on their fluency and inflection; after the teacher reads the story using proper expression, students read it in unison mimicking expressions

computer literate – the ability at some level to understand and use computers

deductive learning – learning that proceeds from the general to the specific; see expository learning

dialog journal – an informal written conversation between two or more people (student-student or student-teacher) about topics of mutual interest.

differentiated instruction – an approach to teaching and learning based on the premise that instructional approaches should vary and be adapted to the needs of individual and diverse students in the classroom

digital native – a person born in the age of computer technology

direct instruction – a form of teacher-centered instruction in which goals are clear and the teacher controls the materials and the pace

discovery learning – learning that proceeds from identification of a problem, through the development and testing of the hypotheses, to the arrival at a conclusion

ELL – English Language Learner

ESE – Exceptional Student Education

ESOL – English for Speakers of Other Languages

essential question – sets the focus for the lesson; the objective in the form of a question

ethnicity – a term used to describe the cultural characteristics of people who identify themselves with a particular ethnic group

formative assessment – the assessment of a student's progress at regular intervals for the purpose of improving the student's achievement

gifted – a category of special needs characterized by unusually high ability in one or more areas, to the point where students require special educational services to meet their full potential

guided practice – an opportunity for each student to demonstrate grasp of new learning by working through an activity or exercise under the direct supervision of the teacher

IDEA (Individuals with Disabilities Education Act) – a federal law ensuring services to children with disabilities; governs how states and public agencies provide early intervention, special education, and related services to eligible students with disabilities

IEP (Individual Education Plan) – mandated by Individuals with Disabilities Education Act; schools are required to develop a plan to meet the needs of all students who meet federal and state requirements for special education

independent practice – students are provided time to reinforce the content or skill previously mastered so that the learning is not forgotten

indirect instruction – the role of the teacher shifts from lecturer/director to that of facilitator, supporter, and resource person; teaching strategies emphasize concept learning, inquiry, and problem solving

indirect teaching – student-centered teaching using discovery and inquiry instructional strategies

inductive learning – learning that proceeds from specifics to the general; see discovery learning

inquiry learning – like discovery learning except the learner designs the processes to be used in resolving the problem, thereby requiring higher levels of cognition

jigsaw – a cooperative learning strategy in which class is divided into groups; each member of group is given a part of an assignment; members of group report their findings to rest of group

K-W-L –type of graphic organizer that charts what the students know, what they want to learn, and what they have learned; **K** and **W** are completed by students before the lesson is taught

learning modality – the way a person receives information; four modalities are recognized: visual, auditory, tactile (touch), and kinesthetic (movement)

learning style – the way a person learns best in a given situation

LEP – Limited English Proficiency

manipulative – type of object that can be manipulated to help the tactile student learn; examples are Unifix cubes and clocks

mastery learning – the concept that a student should master the content of one lesson before moving on to the content of the next

META Agreement – (Florida Consent Decree, 1990) agreement between the Florida State Board Of Education and Multicultural Education, Training and Advocacy, Inc. (META) to provide adequate and appropriate education to non-English speaking students

multiculturalism – a recognition that ethnic groups make up and contribute to a national culture while they maintain an individual identity

multiple intelligences – Howard Gardner's theory of nine distinct intelligences or talents

multiple question – two or more questions asked at one time without allowing the student think-time to answer the first question

peer buddy – partnering students together to help each other

performance objective – *see* behavioral objective

questioning – the act of asking questions as a tactic of instruction

reciprocal teaching – a form of collaborative teaching where the teacher and the students share the teaching responsibility and all are involved in asking questions, clarifying, predicting, and summarizing

Section 504 – protects all persons with a disability who (1) have a physical or mental impairment, which substantially limits one or more major life activities; (2) have a record of such impairment; or (3) are regarded as having such impairments

socio- economic status (SES) – relative standing in society as measured by variables such as income, occupation, education, access to health coverage and community resources, and political power and prestige

SQ3R – survey, question, read, recite, review; study method in which student glances over material (survey), wonders what the material might answer (question), reads the material with a purpose, recites key concepts, and reviews or assesses self for comprehension

Story map – a type of graphic organizer that helps students analyze or write a story

T- chart – a type of graphic organizer chart used to compare and contrast events, people, ideas, etc., by placing individual characteristics in either the left or right section

TESOL – Teachers of English to Speakers of Other Languages

think/pair/share – a learning strategy in which the teacher poses a problem, gives the students time to think of a solution, pairs up the students to solve the solution together, then randomly chooses students to report their findings

Venn Diagram – type of graphic organizer that compares two or more objects; each circle includes attributes of the individual object; where the circles intersect include the object's commonalities

wait-time – in the use of questioning, the period of silence between the time a question is asked and the questioner (teacher) does something, such as repeating the question, rephrasing the question, calling on a particular student, answering the question, or asking another question

wait time avoidance – the time when a student has completed an activity and is waiting for the next activity

WHY WE KNOW...

Research

Academic standards form the framework of the curriculum by identifying the concepts, ideas, and skills that should be taught in each subject area and at each grade level. Research has shown that effective teachers focus on the purpose of the lesson—the standard. The federal No Child Left Behind Act (NCLB) of 2001 requires states to establish high academic standards of what students should know and be able to do in reading, math, and science.

FLORIDA SUNSHINE STATE STANDARDS

The Florida Board of Education created the Sunshine State Standards in 1996 to improve student achievement among the state's students. The purpose of the standards was to provide school districts with the flexibility in designing curriculum. Grade Level Expectations were later added to the standards when the Florida legislature demanded districts be held more accountable for improving student achievement.

The No Child Left Behind Act of 2001, which required states to develop and implement curriculum content standards to close the achievement gap between subgroups of students, resulted in a review of Florida's standards. On July 1, 2008, the Florida legislature instructed the Board of Education to review the Sunshine State Standards and replace them with the Next Generation Sunshine State Standards.

GOAL 3 STANDARDS

In addition to the Next Generation Sunshine State Standards, Florida teachers are responsible for supporting the state's School-to-Work initiatives, also known as the Goal 3 Standards. Instruction in all subject areas and at all grade levels must provide students with the competencies needed for successful work job performance.

The Goal 3 Standards (Florida Department of Education, 1998) include:

Standard 1: Information Managers*
Florida students locate, comprehend, interpret, evaluate, maintain, and apply information, concepts, and ideas found in literature, the arts, symbols, recordings, video and other graphic displays, and computer files in order to perform tasks and/or for enjoyment.

Standard 2: Effective Communication*
Florida students communicate in English and other languages using information, concepts, prose, symbols, reports, audio and video recordings, speeches, graphic displays, and computer-based programs.

Standard 3: Numeric Problem Solvers*
Florida students use numeric operations and concepts to describe, analyze, communicate, synthesize numeric data, and to identify and solve problems.

Standard 4: Creative & Critical Thinkers*
Florida students use creative thinking skills to generate new ideas, make the best decision, recognize and solve problems through reasoning, interpret symbolic data, and develop efficient techniques for lifelong learning.

Standard 5:   Responsible Workers
Florida students display responsibility, self-esteem, sociability, self-management, integrity, and honesty.

Standard 6: Allocate Time, Money, Materials, etc.
Florida students will appropriately allocate time, money, materials, and other resources.

Standard 7: Systems Managers
Florida students integrate their knowledge and understanding of how social, organizational, informational, and technological systems work with their abilities to analyze trends, design and improve systems, and use and maintain appropriate technology.

Standard 8: Cooperative Workers
Florida students work cooperatively to successfully complete a project or activity.

Standard 9: Effective Learners
Florida students establish credibility with their colleagues through competence and integrity and help their peers achieve their goals by communicating their feelings and ideas to justify or successfully negotiate a position which advances goal attainment.

Standard 10: Multicultural Sensitive Citizens
Florida students appreciate their own culture and the cultures of others, understand the concerns and perspectives of members of other ethnic and gender groups, reject the stereotyping of themselves and others, and seek out and utilize the views of persons from diverse ethnic, social, and educational backgrounds while completing individual and group projects.

Standard 11: Involvement of Families
Families will share the responsibility of accomplishing the standards set in Goal 3 throughout a student's education from preschool through adult.

(* tested on state assessment exams)

Grade levels and focus for Goal 3 Standards are listed below:

GRADE LEVEL	FOCUS
Pre-Kindergarten – Grade 2	Awareness
Grades 3 - 5	Orientation
Grades 6 - 8	Exploration
Grades 9 - 12	Preliminary Career Focus

FLORIDA MULTICULTURAL MANDATES

Teachers in Florida are not only required to teach the Florida Sunshine Standards and Goal 3 Standards, they must also incorporate the state's Multicultural Mandates in their lesson plans.

In 1994, the Florida Legislature passed Florida Statute 1003.42 requiring public schools to teach "the history of the Holocaust (1933-1945)" for the purpose of encouraging tolerance of diversity. The statute was amended that same year requiring schools to include the contributions of African-Americans to the United States. In 1998, the statute was further amended to include the contributions of Hispanics and women.

In 2004, each school district was required to implement a character development program that stressed the qualities of patriotism, responsibility, citizenship, kindness, respect, honesty, self-control, tolerance, and cooperation in kindergarten through grade 12 (State of Florida, 2010).

WHAT YOU NEED TO KNOW...

In order for students to learn, teachers need to provide learning experiences that make subject content meaningful. These experiences must take into account student interest and motivation to learn, incentives for learning, and means for engaging the student in the learning process (Jalongo, 2007).

Teachers can encourage _student interest_ and _motivation_ to learn by:
- linking prior student knowledge to new information,
- providing students with opportunities to apply their application of prior and new knowledge,
- capturing student interest before the lesson begins,
- engaging students in the learning process,
- giving useful feedback, and
- correcting misconceptions.

Teachers can encourage student achievement by providing intrinsic and extrinsic rewards as _incentives for learning_ when students demonstrate competence. These rewards include:
- positive feedback on student work,
- verbal praise, and
- higher grades.

Teachers can _engage students in the learning process_ by:
- selecting interesting and relevant materials,
- demonstrating the teacher's own interest in the lesson content,
- connecting the lesson to the students' own lives,
- asking lower order questions to check for comprehension throughout the lesson,
- increasing the use of higher order questioning to enhance critical thinking,
- providing opportunities for hands-on application of concepts and skills, and
- connecting the new information to what the students already know – their prior knowledge. Routinely assessing student knowledge before introducing new concepts can improve understanding of the new material (Sullo, 2007).

LESSON PLANS

Teachers create lesson plans to communicate their instructional goals regarding specific subject matter. Lesson plans contain student learning objectives, instructional procedures, the required materials, and a written description of how the students will be assessed. Although experienced teachers often reduce lesson plans to a mental map or short outline, new teachers will find detailed lesson plans to be indispensable.

Teachers plan for several reasons. These include ensuring:
- Florida Next Generation Sunshine State Standards and Goal 3 Standards are covered and align with lesson objectives
- strategies and activities meet the needs of all students,
- procedures are established to minimize control problems,
- lesson continuation (plan can be used by substitute if teacher is absent), and
- self-evaluation and reflection ("Did students learn what I wanted them to learn?").

STEPS FOR WRITING A LESSON PLAN

Step 1: Identify the Subject Matter Content
- Indicate what you intend to teach.
- Identify which forms of knowledge (concept, academic rule, skill, law, law-like principles, and/or value knowledge) will be included in the lesson (see Chapter 3).
- Give a full description of the forms of knowledge you will be using. If you plan to present the information as a concept, identify the concept, define it, list attributes, and give examples and non-examples. If you plan to present the information as an academic rule, identify the rule and when or where it must be applied.   Do the same with laws, law-like principles, and value knowledge.
- Identify and define new vocabulary words.

Step 2: Write the Instructional Objective(s)/Outcomes
- Indicate what is to be learned. Ask yourself, "What do I want my students to master and be able to do at the end of the lesson? How will I measure that this was achieved?"
- Identify the Florida Sunshine State Standard(s) and benchmarks assessed in the lesson. (What are the expectations of the standard?)
- Identify the activities in the lesson linked to the *Goal 3 Standards*.
- Write SMART lesson objectives (Specific Content, Measurable Outcome, Attainable Action Verb, Resources, Time).

Example of a SMART Objective:

Given a map, the student will identify with 90% accuracy the states aligned with the Union or the Confederacy in a 15-minute activity.

> **S** = states that were aligned with the Union or the Confederacy
> **M** = 90% accuracy
> **A** = identify
> **R** = map
> **T** = 15-minute activity

Note: If a student fails to identify 90% of the Union and Confederate states on a map, the student has not achieved the teacher's objective for the lesson.

Example of a SMART Objective:

After reading "Clifford the Big Red Dog," the student will be able to describe the plot of the story with 100% accuracy by the end of the 20-minute reading activity.

> S = plot of a story
> M = 100% accuracy
> A = describe
> R = "Clifford the Big Red Dog" book
> T = 20-minute reading activity

Note: If a student fails to describe the plot of "Clifford the Big Red Dog" accurately, the student has not achieved the teacher's objective for the lesson.

Non-Example:

The student will understand how to solve simple addition problems.

> **S** = addition problems
> **M** = *(missing)*
> **A** = *(missing—how do you know they "understand"?)*
> **R** = *(missing)*
> **T** = *(missing)*

Note: This is not a SMART objective. How will the student demonstrate solving simple addition problems (<u>attainable action verb</u>)? What <u>resources</u> will be used (teacher demonstration? worksheets?). How many problems need to be correct (<u>measurement</u>) to determine if the student can solve simple addition problems? How much <u>time</u> should it take the student to demonstrate mastery of solving simple addition problems? (Never use "understand," "learn," or "know" in objectives since they are general terms rather than specific measureable outcomes.)

Step 3: Identify the Instructional Procedures

- Indicate how you intend to sequence the activities in the lesson from initiation to closure.
- Estimate the time needed to complete each major component of the lesson. Include these three major components:
    1. Lesson Initiating Activity
    2. Core Activities (Directed, Guided Practice, and/or Independent Activity)
    3. Closure Activity
- List the questions you will ask your students throughout the lesson, identifying high/low levels.   The levels should vary.
- Incorporate instructional procedures that address the needs of diverse learners (ESE, LEP) and different learning styles.
- Describe the classroom management procedures, including seating arrangements, which will effectively facilitate the delivery of the lesson.

Step 4: List the Materials and Equipment Needed for the Lesson

- List all materials and equipment used by both the teacher and the learner.

Step 5: Identify the Assessment/ Evaluation Techniques

- Identify the techniques to be used to determine whether the students have attained each instructional objective (for example: tests, presentations, products, and/or systematic observation).
- Specify how the needs of diverse learners will be accommodated according to language level, disability, and/or learning styles.

LESSON DELIVERY OPTIONS

Beginning of the Lesson:
The beginning of a lesson should include lesson-initiating activities that last 5 – 15 minutes. This section provides answers to the following questions:
- What do the students know?
- What will they learn today?
- Why is it important to learn the material?

Some activity options include:
- reviewing the previous day's lesson by asking questions,
- gaining the students' attention by introducing a story or an attention-grabbing article, and
- using a graphic organizer to determine prior knowledge.

Middle of the Lesson:
The middle of the lesson should include core activities that last 30 – 45 minutes. This section includes:
- instructional delivery,
- engaging students in the learning process, and
- asking high and low order questions.

Some activity options include:
- lecture,
- cooperative groups,
- student presentations,
- small group activities,
- individual seat work,
- multi-media presentations,
- graphic organizers,
- games, and
- centers.

End of the Lesson:
The end of the lesson should include closure activities that last 5 – 15 minutes. This section provides answers to the following questions:
- What did the students learn today?
- How well did the students learn it?
- How will I assess the students?

Some activity options include:
- lesson review,
- demonstration of skills,
- post-test,
- written feedback,
- group processing, and
- questions with corrective feedback.

USING DATA TO EVALUATE LEARNING OUTCOMES

Teachers can use a variety of data to evaluate the effectiveness of their lessons. The data can include formative assessments, as well as data collected by colleagues observing the lesson taught. Strategies to improve effectiveness of lesson presentations include:
- Modeling – After identifying an objective on which students earned low scores, a teacher leader can model an instructional strategy that has proven to be effective.
- Resources – Colleagues can identify additional resources the teacher can use to re-teach an objective the students failed to learn.
- Grouping – The teacher can identify students who share common weaknesses and review the material with those students (Matthews, Trimble, & Gay, 2007),

FORMATIVE ASSESSMENTS

Formative assessments, as part of the instructional process, provide immediate feedback to the teacher regarding student learning during the lesson. The assessments let the teacher know if the lesson was taught well or if instruction needs to be modified based on the students' level of understanding. Additionally, formative assessments provide students with evidence of their own current learning progress (Chappuis, & Chappuis, 2008). Examples of formative assessments include:
- asking questions during the lesson to check for understanding,
- observing students while they are working,
- asking students to summarize the key idea of the lesson in one sentence (One Sentence Summary), and
- asking students to write down the most significant fact they learned during the lesson (Minute Paper).

ASKING QUESTIONS DURING A LESSON

There are five steps effective teachers follow when asking questions during a lesson. They are:

Step 1: Ask the question. Be sure to vary the level of the question (low and high order).

Step 2: Pause three seconds to enable students to think about their response.

Step 3: Call on a student to answer the question.

Step 4: Pause one or two seconds for students to process the answer they heard.

Step 5: Acknowledge/respond to the student by repeating the answer, rephrasing the answer, giving a corrective, or making a positive comment on the response of the student.

Teachers must always respond to the answers students give, even if the answers are incorrect. If corrections are not given, students will repeat their mistakes.

When asking questions, effective teachers:

Avoid Multiple Questions—Ask one question at a time; wait for response; ask second question. Asking more than one question at a time can make it difficult for students to focus on the questions. They may remember the easiest question or only the last question they hear.

Non-Example: "What is 50% of 10 and 75% of 16?"
Example: "What is 50% of 10?" *(Teacher calls on student and acknowledges response.)* "What is 75% of 16?" *(Teacher calls on student and acknowledges response.)*

Ask Precise Questions—Ask a question using as few words as possible. Asking a long question can confuse students as to the information the teacher is trying to elicit.

Non-Example: "What was the theory of natural selection formulated by Charles Darwin after he was puzzled by the geographical distribution of wildlife and fossils collected on his voyage in 1838?"
Example: "What is Charles Darwin's theory of natural selection?"

USING DIFFERENTIATED INSTRUCTION TO IMPROVE
THE QUALITY OF INSTRUCTION

We are all aware of the diversity that exists in the modern classroom. Not all students are alike—they come from many different cultures, countries, and backgrounds. Some students also have special needs and different learning styles. Effective teachers need to approach teaching and learning based on the premise that instructional methods and activities should vary according to these needs. This theory is referred to as Differentiated Instruction.

Differentiated Instruction is based on the premise that teachers should adjust their instructional approaches to meet the needs of all students in the classroom. There are three elements of the curriculum that can be differentiated: Content, Process, and Products (Tomlinson, 2001). While students vary in their readiness, teachers using different content, processes, and products can help all their students learn.

Teachers using differentiated instruction need to:

1. identify their students' specific needs;

2. be flexible;

3. offer instruction that blends whole-class, group, and individual instruction;

4. keep the focus on concepts, not the memorization of fragmented facts;

5. address the same concepts for all students, but adjust the degree of complexity based on the needs of the individual learners;

6. expect learners to interact and work together as they learn;

7. allow students to provide varied types of products;

8. provide a balance between teacher-assigned and student-selected tasks;

9. assess students frequently;

10. identify students who need more support and those who can leap forward (not all students need a certain task); and

11. recognize the learning style of their students.

Examples of Differentiated Instruction in the Classroom

Topic of lesson: Civil Rights Movement

Traditional Method of Instruction:
The teacher *lectures* about the Civil Rights movement. Students *take notes* and turn in a report based on a *topic assigned by the teacher*. After a *test*, the teacher moves on to the next topic.

Differentiated Instruction:
The teacher presents the concept of Civil Rights using a *media footage of actual events*. *Students are given a choice* of writing a report on a Civil Rights leader during the 1960s, acting out a scene in "Raisin in the Sun," writing a rap song about the Civil Rights movement, or creating a timeline on a poster. *Students work in pairs, groups, or independently*. *Teacher frequently assesses students* by questioning them as they work on their projects.

Topic of lesson: Planets in the Solar System

Traditional Method of Instruction:
The teacher tells the students to *read* about the solar system in their textbook. After they have completed reading the chapter, they are *given a worksheet*. The teacher gives a *quiz* on the chapter.

Differentiated Instruction:
The teacher presents a *PowerPoint presentation* on the concept of the planets and the solar system. Students are assigned to *Cooperative Learning Groups.* Each group is assigned a planet and must *create a styrofoam model of the planet and its relationship to Earth*. Groups must also prepare a report on their assigned planet and *present the report to the class, using posters and graphics*. The teacher uses *rubrics to assess the groups.*

MULTIPLE INTELLIGENCES & DIFFERENTIATED INSTRUCTION

In 1983, Dr. Howard Gardner proposed that learners have multiple intelligences—linguistic, logical-mathematical, spatial, bodily-kinesthetic, musical, interpersonal, intrapersonal, naturalist, and existential. A description of each intelligence is listed below (Hoerr, 1996; McCoog, 2010).

- **Spatial** – ability to visualize; learns best by seeing the presentations
- **Linguistic** – ability with words both written and spoken; learns best by reading, listening to lectures, taking notes, and discussions
- **Logical-Mathematical** – ability to reason; can use logic, think abstractly, and is good with numbers
- **Kinesthetic** – ability to learn things through the body; has muscle memory; learns best by doing through movement, physically constructing, dancing, and physical activity
- **Musical** – sensitive to sounds and music; learns best through songs and rhythms; lectures may be choice of lesson delivery
- **Interpersonal** – ability to interact with others; learns best by working cooperatively in groups
- **Intrapersonal** – ability to be self-reflective and intuitive; works best alone
- **Naturalist** – ability to relate information to one's natural surroundings
- **Existential** – ability to question the reason for existence

According to Gardner, schools were only focusing on linguistic intelligence and logical-mathematical intelligence. He suggested that teachers present lessons in a wide variety of methods using music, cooperative learning, art, role-playing, multimedia, inner reflection, field trips, graphic arts, technology, and much more.

SOCIO-ECONOMIC STATUS AND LEARNING

Research has indicated that low socio-economic status (SES) and academic achievement are related. Teachers should take into account the following when working with students from these communities.

SES & Student Preparation for School

- Many students fall behind academically and never catch up.
- Others begin school far behind their peers of generally higher socio-economic status.
- Students are usually below grade level in vocabulary, reading, and math.
- Parents do not have the resources to provide enrichment activities (trips to museums, etc.).

SES & Student Attendance

- Students may be frequently absent because they have family responsibilities (babysitting, second job, etc.).
- Failures in school may result in skipping classes to avoid embarrassment.

SES & Families of Students

- Family members lack confidence in their own knowledge and skills.
- Parents perceive schools as cold, hierarchical institutions; they do not feel liked, respected, or valued.
- Parents' roles and responsibilities in the education of their children vary due to cultural and/or socio-economic factors.

What Teachers Can Do

- Communicate with Parents:
    - Let the parents know you are interested in helping their student.
    - Invite parents to meet with you or to call you if they have any questions or concerns.

- Encourage Students:
    - Provide student with remedial work when necessary.
    - Provide enrichment activities in areas in which student excels.

- Student Activities:
    - Identify the interests of the student (art, music, sports, etc.).
    - Provide students with engaging activities.

LIMITED ENGLISH PROFICIENT (LEP) STUDENTS AND LEARNING

In 2005, 4.13 million Florida residents over the age of five reported they spoke a language other than English at home. This represents about 25.8% of Florida's population. Of those residents, 11.7% stated they spoke English "less than very well" (U.S. Census Bureau, 2008).

Teachers need to be sensitive to the needs of Limited English Speaking (LEP) students. Many immigrant and refugee parents do not ask about the curriculum for their children. Instead, they respect teachers as authority figures and expect them to use appropriate strategies to help students reach their academic potential (Vang, 2006).

Classification of Limited English Proficiency Students

When a student is enrolled in a school, a home language survey is administered to the parent to determine whether:
- a language other than English is used in the home,
- the student has a first language other than English, and
- the student most frequently speaks a language other than English.

Based on the answers provided by the parent, a language proficiency test is administered in the areas of:
- listening comprehension (understanding),
- speaking,
- reading, and
- writing.

Students are placed in an LEP category based on their assessment results. The No Child Left Behind (NCLB) Act requires schools to test their LEP students in reading, math, and science and be accountable for the results.

FLORIDA LEP LANGUAGE LEVEL CLASSIFICATIONS & DESCRIPTIONS

LEP students differ according to their levels of English proficiency. The assistance they receive is based on their language classifications (Florida Department of State, 2010). The categories are:

LANGUAGE PROFICIENCY CLASSIFICATION	LANGUAGE CATEGORY DESCRIPTION
A	**Non-English Speaker** • Monolingual speaker of a language other than English • Cannot communicate meaning orally or communicates in English with one or two-word responses • Unable to participate in regular classroom instruction
B	**Intermediate English Speaker** • Predominantly speaks language other than English • Communicates orally in English with mostly simple phrases and/or sentence responses; may lack academic language terminology • Makes significant grammatical errors that interfere with understanding • Experiences some difficulty in following grade level subject matter assignments
C	**Advanced English Speaker** • Understands and speaks English fairly well or with near fluency; bilingual • Makes occasional grammatical errors • May read and write English with variant degrees of proficiency
D	**Full English Speaker** • Speaks English fluently • Reads and writes English at a comparable level with English-speaking counterparts
E	**Monolingual English Speaker** • Fully English speaking
F	**Monolingual English Speaker** • Fully English proficient

What Teachers Can Do

Instructional modifications for LEP students should be based the level of the student's English proficiency. Modifications include:
- using bilingual dictionaries,
- providing bilingual support,
- utilizing one-on-one instruction with the teacher,
- providing meaningful language practice,
- using illustrations and diagrams,
- paraphrasing and using repetition as needed,
- using simple language,
- varying the complexity of the assignment,
- modifying the type of the assignment,
- substituting a diagram for a paragraph, and
- using all learning styles.

When teaching vocabulary to LEP students, teachers should remember to:
- explain key concepts,
- use Interactive Word Walls,
- provide context clues,
- categorize the vocabulary,
- use Word Banks,
- limit the use of idioms, and
- match visuals with the new vocabulary.

Visuals, graphic organizers, and audio materials have proven to be successful when teaching LEP students.   The chart below gives examples in each category.

VISUALS	GRAPHIC ORGANIZERS	AUDIO
Labeling Maps Pictures Computer/Software Video with captioning Manipulatives	Charts Flow Charts Graphs K-W-L Story Maps T-Charts Timelines Venn Diagrams	Audio Books Computer/Software Music on CDs

Which LEP Instructional Strategies Should Teachers Use?

Teachers must use instructional strategies that are appropriate for the English speaking ability of their students. Strategies that have proven to be effective include:

- Choral Reading
- Dialogue Journals
- Games
- Jigsaw
- Peer Buddy
- Role Playing
- Think/Pair/Share
- Word Banks
- Demonstrations
- Field Trips
- Group Projects/Group Reports
- Note Taking/Outline Notes
- Read Aloud
- Think Aloud
- Summarizing
- SQ3R (Survey, Question, Read, Recite, Review

Which Type of Assessments Should Teachers Use?

In addition to traditional assessments such as tests, teachers of LEP students should consider using alternative assessment methods such as checklists, interviews, observation, portfolios, rubrics, retelling, and writing samples.

How do Students Exit the LEP Program?

The U.S. Department of Education's Office of English Language Acquisition has ruled that students must be proficient on a state's LEP assessment and meet any other criteria used by the state in order to exit the program (U.S. Department of Education, 2008).

EXCEPTIONAL STUDENT EDUCATION (ESE) STUDENTS AND LEARNING

School Districts must provide education programs for students ages three through 21 who have disabilities or who are gifted. The 2004 Individuals with Disabilities Education Act (IDEA) is the law that requires schools to provide special education services to eligible students with disabilities. IDEA also requires an Individual Education Plan (IEP) be developed and provided to each eligible child. The IEP is the blueprint for the student's educational program and identifies the student's educational goals, services to be provided, and evaluation criteria. There are 14 categories of disabilities addressed under IDEA (Knoblauch & Sorenson, 1998).

Categories of Special Education Disabilities Addressed Under IDEA

- **Autism Spectrum**—a developmental disability that affects verbal and nonverbal communication as well as social interaction; characteristics are repetitive activities, stereotyped movements, resistance to change in daily routines, and unusual responses to sensory experiences.

- **Deaf-Blindness**—combined hearing and visual impairments that cause severe communication problems

- **Deafness**—hearing is so impaired that child cannot process linguistic information with or without amplification

- **Developmentally Delayed** (ages 3-9 only)—a young child who is exhibiting significant delays in physical development (motor skills), cognitive development (intellectual abilities), communication development (language and speech), social or emotional development (emotional control and social skills), and/or adaptive development (self-care skills)

- **Emotional Disturbance**—a condition with one or more of the following characteristics: (1) inappropriate types of behavior or feelings; (2) an inability to learn that cannot be explained by health, intellectual or sensory factors; (3) inability to build appropriate interpersonal relationships with peers or adults; (4) a pervasive mood of depression or unhappiness; or (5) a development of fears or physical symptoms associated with personal or school problems

- **Hearing Impairment**—impairment in hearing that is not included under the definition of deafness

- **Intellectual Disability** (Educable, Trainable, Profound)—significantly below average intellectual functioning with deficits in adaptive behavior, manifested during the child's developmental period

- **Multiple Disabilities**—simultaneous impairments (such as profound intellectual disability and blindness); combination of impairments cause severe educational needs that cannot be accommodated in a program solely for one of the impairments.

- **Orthopedic Impairment**—impairments caused by a congenital anomaly, disease, or from other causes (amputations, burns, etc.)

- **Other Health Impairment**—child has chronic or acute health problems (heart condition, leukemia, etc.) that adversely affect child's educational performance

- **Specific Learning Disability**—a disorder in one or more of the processes involved in using language; student is unable to perfectly listen, think, speak, read, write, spell or calculate; includes dyslexia; does not include problems that are the result of hearing, motor, or visual disabilities

- **Speech or Language Impairment**—includes stuttering or impaired articulation

- **Traumatic Brain Injury**—physical injury to the brain that affects learning, speech, memory, attention, reasoning, judgment, abstract thinking, processing of information, and physical functions

- **Visual Impairment Including Blindness** (Blind/Partially Sighted)—child's vision is impaired, despite efforts at correction

What Teachers Can Do

- Follow the student's IEP (Individual Education Plan)
- Share evaluations of student with parents and the ESE Specialist

Which Strategies Should Teachers Use?

Strategies and modifications for the classroom are usually provided in the student's IEP. The most commonly used are:
- test taking (open book, extra time, oral exam),
- behavior (time out, rewards),
- assignments (check comprehension of directions, reduce length of assignments),
- arrangement of room (hearing or visually impaired, physically disabled), and
- presentation of instruction (peer note taker, computer assisted instruction).

GIFTED STUDENTS

Gifted students are those who have demonstrated remarkably high levels of achievement in the areas of intellect, creativity, art, and leadership when compared to others of their age and experience. They also are in need of services to develop their capabilities. Some gifted students may also have learning disabilities and receive exceptional student education services to address those needs.

Teachers will notice that gifted students:
- are creative, showing original thought and imagination;
- express their emotions with force and conviction;
- are quick to challenge, question, and criticize;
- are capable of understanding complex information;
- may be emotionally immature;
- are perceptive and quick witted; and
- often have a quirky sense of humor.

504 MODIFICATION STUDENTS AND LEARNING

Teachers may have students in their classes who have disabilities that limit their ability to learn in the school environment; yet, they do not meet the more stringent requirements for special education services. Section 504 of the Rehabilitation Act of 1973 is an access law that requires schools to provide reasonable accommodations and adaptations (referred to as 504 Plans) for these students.

A 504 Plan describes the accommodations being made to support the student and may be updated at any time to reflect necessary changes. Examples of students on a 504 Plan are a student who has arthritis and cannot walk up stairs or a student diagnosed with Attention Deficit Disorder.

What Teachers Can Do

- Be involved in the development of the 504 Plan
- Know which of your students have a plan
- Read the plan as soon as possible
- Consult with your school's liaison
- Express any concerns you have about implementing the plan
- Propose alternative accommodations when necessary
- Treat the plan as a legal contract to which you are a party
- Document your implementation of the plan

Which Strategies Should Teachers Use?

Strategies and modifications for the classroom are usually provided in the student's 504 Plan. The most commonly used are:

- giving extra time to complete tasks,
- shortening assignments,
- praising specific behaviors,
- giving extra privileges and rewards,
- cueing student to stay on task,
- pairing student with other students, and
- seating student near the teacher's desk.

DIVERSE LEARNING STYLES

Since students have different learning styles, teachers need to use diverse strategies when presenting instruction. The three major learning styles are Auditory, Visual, and Kinesthetic-Tactile.

Auditory

Students in this category frequently:
- enjoy talking and are seldom quiet,
- have poor handwriting,
- remember spoken words,
- have poor visual memory,
- enjoy class discussions, and
- can be observed reading to self during silent reading.

Visual

Students in this category frequently:
- do better when you show them,
- like pictures and puzzles,
- notice details,
- may rarely talk in class, and
- have trouble learning from lectures.

Kinesthetic-Tactile

Students in this category frequently:
- may be considered hyperactive,
- like to take things apart and put them together,
- learn best by doing and exploring, and
- lose interest when not actively involved.

According to William Glasser, we learn:

10% of what we **Read**	20% of what we **Hear**	30% of what we **See & Hear**	50% of what we **Discuss** with others	70% of what we **Experience** with others	90% of what we **Teach** others
	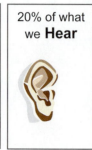	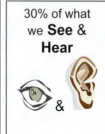			

NEUROLOGICAL PROFILING

Beliefs, the choices made, and how individuals think are all guided by neurological strengths and weaknesses. This affects teaching styles and how students learn. In order to reach all students, teachers need to be aware of their dominant side as well as the dominant sides of their students (Connell, 2002).

Right-Brain Dominant

- Intuitive and emotional
- Teacher's attributes:
    - Prefers hands-on activities
    - Incorporates visuals and music in lessons
    - Assigns group projects
    - Prefers an active, noisy classroom
    - Supplies a vast amount of materials in the classroom for the students to utilize
- Student's attributes:
    - Prefers to work in groups
    - Enjoys art projects over writing papers
    - Thinks in pictures

Left-Brain Dominant

- Sequential and time oriented
- Teacher's attributes:
    - Prefers to lecture
    - Assigns more independent research and writing
    - Prefers a quiet structured classroom
    - Likes everything in its place
- Student's attributes:
    - Prefers to work independently
    - Does not like distractions
    - Likes order
    - Tends to be perfectionist

Middle Brain Dominant

More flexible than the right and left-brain dominants but fluctuates between the two when it comes to decision making.

LET IT SHOW!

Below is a list of different methods you can use to demonstrate your accomplishment of **FEAP #1: INSTRUCTIONAL DESIGN AND LESSON PLANNING**.

(a) Aligns instruction with state-adopted standards at the appropriate level of rigor
- ▶ Use state-adopted standards aligned with objectives for all lessons.
- ▶ Use the Internet/Intranet: Download a lesson plan you can use from the Internet or Intranet. Align the lesson with the appropriate state adopted standards and make sure the lesson's degree of difficulty is appropriate for your students.

(b) Sequences lessons and concepts to ensure coherence and required prior knowledge
- ▶ Plan lesson initiating activities or beginning reviews to link prior knowledge to new concepts and skills.
- ▶ Create a Lesson: Create a lesson that requires your students to gather information and solve a problem.

(c) Designs instruction for students to achieve mastery
- ▶ Use data from teacher-made, district, and/or state assessments to determine students' strengths and weaknesses. Use the data to identify the best methods for remediation.
- ▶ Create a Lesson: Create a lesson that utilizes strategies for your visual, audio, and kinesthetic/tactile learners.
- ▶ Analyze State Assessment Data: Review the previous year's state assessment results for your students. Identify your students who need remediation in each strand. Create activities that will help remediate your students.

(d) Selects appropriate formative assessments to monitor learning
- ▶ Create Questions for Your Lesson Plan: Prepare a good balance of low and high order questions to ask students during your lesson plan.
- ▶ Create a Quiz: Create a short quiz that assesses your students' mastery of your lesson's objectives.
- ▶ Create a "ticket out the door" comprehension check.

(e) Uses a variety of data, independently, and in collaboration with colleagues, to evaluate learning outcomes, adjust planning and continuously improve the effectiveness of the lessons
- ▶ Create a pretest or activity to determine prior knowledge. Use the data to drive your instruction.
- ▶ Attend an IEP Meeting: Participate in an IEP meeting for one of your ESE students and help develop the student's learning goals for your class.
- ▶ Plan with Colleagues: Work with your colleagues to create a lesson plan that meets the needs of your LEP students.

▶ Develop a Unit Plan: After conducting a thorough data analysis of prior test data, plan lessons within a unit emphasizing areas of concern. Group students according to the areas of skill improvement as indicated from the data analysis.

(f) Develops learning experiences that require students to demonstrate a variety of applicable skills and competencies

▶ Develop an Instructional Activity: Develop an instructional activity in which students utilize technology.

▶ Create a Lesson: Create a lesson in which your students will have to predict or create a hypothesis.

▶ Create a Lesson: Demonstrate your ability to create lessons that require students to research diverse points of view.

▶ Develop an academic service-learning project for students to work in the community to apply what they are learning in class.

ACTIVITY OVERVIEW FOR DEMONSTRATING PROFICIENCY IN
<u>FEAP #1: INSTRUCTIONAL DESIGN AND LESSON PLANNING</u>

(a) Aligns instruction with state-adopted standards at the appropriate level of rigor

   Activity B: LESSON PLAN

(b) Sequences lessons and concepts to ensure coherence and required prior knowledge

   Activity B: LESSON PLAN

(c) Designs instruction for students to achieve mastery

   Activity A: WRITING <u>SMART</u> INSTRUCTIONAL OBJECTIVES
   Activity B: LESSON PLAN
   Activity D: ACTIVITIES TO MASTER LESSON OBJECTIVES

(d) Selects appropriate formative assessments to monitor learning

   Activity B: LESSON PLAN

(e) Uses diagnostic student data to plan lessons

   Activity B: LESSON PLAN
   Activity C: LEARNING STYLES

(f) Develops learning experiences that require students to demonstrate a variety of applicable skills and competencies

   Activity B: LESSON PLAN

ACTIVITY A

WRITING <u>SMART</u> INSTRUCTIONAL OBJECTIVES (FEAP 1)

The five components of a SMART objective are: **S**pecific Content, **M**easurable Outcome, **A**ttainable Action, **R**esource, and **T**ime Frame.

<u>Example</u>: By the end of this lesson, using the diagram provided, students will be able to label correctly three out of the four parts of a plant during seven minutes of independent seatwork.

> **S**—parts of the plant
> **M**—3 out of 4
> **A**—label
> **R**—diagram
> **T**—seven minutes of independent seatwork

<u>Part 1</u>. Identify the components in the following objectives.

1. By the end of a 20-minute independent practice, students will be able to order 10 fractions with like and unlike denominators on the worksheet provided with 80% accuracy.

> **S**—
> **M**—
> **A**—
> **R**—
> **T**—

2. By the end of a lecture/discussion on the causes and effects of the Civil War, students will explain in writing at least two causes of the war and its impact on landowners during 11 minutes of independent seatwork.

> **S**—
> **M**—
> **A**—
> **R**—
> **T**—

<u>Part 2</u>. Develop your own SMART objective in the space below.

_____

_____

_____

Is your objective SMART? Check by identifying the parts below.

> **S**—
> **M**—
> **A**—
> **R**—
> **T**—

ACTIVITY B

LESSON PLAN (FEAP 1)

Directions: Use this lesson plan template to create a lesson.

Teacher: _____ Date: _____

Subject/Topic: _____ Grade Level: _____ Length of Lesson: _____

I. <u>Subject Matter Content:</u>

What I intend to teach:

Forms of Knowledge:

New Vocabulary words and the definitions:

II. <u>Instructional Objective(s)/Outcomes:</u>

SMART Objective #1:

   1. Sunshine State Standard:

   2. Goal 3 Standard(s):

SMART Objective #2:

   1. Sunshine State Standard:

   2. Goal 3 Standard(s):

III. <u>Instructional Procedures:</u>

Lesson Initiating Activity: Estimated Time_____

Core Activities: Estimated Time_____
   (Directed / Guided Practice / Independent Activity)

Closure Activity: Estimated Time_____

Lower order questions I will ask:

Higher order student questions I will ask:

ESE:
    Classifications of student(s):
    ESE Strategies for this lesson:

ESOL:
    Classifications of student(s):
    ESOL Strategies for this lesson:

Classroom Management Procedures to enhance learning:

IV. <u>Materials and Equipment</u>:

Materials/Equipment used by the Teacher:

Materials/Equipment used by the Learner:

V. <u>Formative Assessment(s)/Evaluation</u>:

Does the formative assessment evaluate student achievement of the SMART objective?

ACTIVITY C

LEARNING STYLES (FEAP 1)

Search the Internet for a learning styles inventory. Administer the inventory to your class and take it yourself. After you have identified your learning style, reflect on the following questions.

1. How do your results affect the way you teach?

2. What data do you have that identifies specific learning needs of your students?

3. How can you change your instruction to meet the learning styles and needs of your students?

ACTIVITY D

ACTIVITIES TO MASTER LESSON OBJECTIVES (FEAP 1)

The purpose of this activity is to use an instructional technique (cooperative learning, inquiry learning, discovery learning, etc.) to create activities you can use in your classroom to help students achieve mastery of the lesson's objective(s).

1. Identify the specific instructional technique.

   _____

2. Give a brief overview of the instructional technique.

   _____

   _____

   _____

Activity # 1

Subject area _____ Grade _____

Name of activity: _____

Write a SMART objective in which this activity can be used.

Describe the activity you have chosen or developed and discuss specifically how you will implement it in your specific subject area.

List materials needed by the student and the teacher.

Explain how this activity will help your students achieve mastery of your lesson's objective(s).

Explain how this activity is related to the instructional technique you selected.

Activity # 2

Subject area _____ Grade _____

Name of activity: _____

Write a SMART objective in which this activity can be used.

Describe the activity you have chosen or developed and discuss specifically how you will implement it in your specific subject area.

List materials needed by the student and the teacher.

Explain how this activity will help your students achieve mastery of your lesson's objective(s).

Explain how this activity is related to the instructional technique you selected.

RESOURCES

Chappuis, S. & Chappuis, J. (2008). The best value in formative assessment. *Educational Leadership*, 65(4), 14-18.

Connell, D. (2002.). Left brain/right brain: Pathways to reach every learner. *Instructor*. 2.28. Retrieved May 10, 2010, from http://cte.dce.harvard.edu/~mdumais/BrainBasedLearningWebsite/Connell_NeuroStrength_Document.doc.pdf

Danielson, C. (2007, 2nd edition). *Enhancing professional practice: A framework for teaching.* Alexandria, VA: Association for Supervision and Curriculum Development.

Distin, K. (2006). *Gifted children: A guide for parents and professionals*. Philadelphia, PA: Jessica Kingsley Publishers.

Florida Department of Education. (2005). *Next generation Sunshine State Standards*. Retrieved May 8, 2010, from http://www.floridastandards.org/Standards/FLStandardSearch.aspx

Florida Department of Education. (1998). *Preparing all learners for tomorrow's workforce.* Retrieved May 8, 2010, from http://www.fldoe.org/workforce/title.asp#Preparing

Florida Department of Education. (2010). *6A-5.065-The Educator Accomplished Practices as approved by the State Board of Education on December 17, 2010.* Retrieved December 21, 2010, from http://www.fldoe.org/profdev/FEAPSRevisions/

Florida Department of State. (2010). *2010-2011 English language learners (ELLs) database and program handbook: English for speakers of other languages.* Retrieved September 6, 2010, from http://www.fldoe.org/aala/pdf/edph1011.pdf

Florida Legislature. (2010). *The 2010 Florida Statutes: Chapter 1003.42—Required Instruction.* Retrieved May 8, 2010, from http://www.leg.state.fl.us/statutes/index.cfm?mode=View%20Statutes&SubMenu=1&App_mode=Display_Statute&Search_String=holocaust&URL=1000-1099/1003/Sections/1003.42.html

Hall, T., Strangman, N. & Meyer, A. (2009). *Differentiated instruction and implications for UDL implementation.* Retrieved June 3, 2010, from http://www.cast.org/publications/ncac/ncac_diffinstruc.html

Hoerr, T. R. (1996). Introducing the theory of multiple intelligences. *NASSP Bulletin*, *80*(583), 8-10.

Individuals with Disabilities Education Act Amendments of 1997. H.R. 5, 105th Cong., 1st Sess. (1997). Retrieved October 8, 2010, from http://www2.ed.gov/policy/speced/leg/idea/idea.pdf

Jalonga, M. R. (2007). Beyond benchmarks and scores: Reasserting the role of motivation and interest in children's academic achievement, an ACEI position paper. *Childhood Education, 83*(6), 395-408.

Knoblauch, B. & Sorenson, B. (1998). *IDEA'S definition of disabilities.* ERIC Clearinghouse on Disabilities and Gifted Education, Reston, VA.

Matthews, J., Trimble, S., & Gay, A. (2007). But what do you do with the data? *The Education Digest, 73*(3), 53-56.

McCoog, I. J. (2010). The existential learner. The Clearing House, 83(4), DOI: 10.1080/00098651003774828

Sullo, R. A. (2007). Activating the desire to learn. Alexandria, VA: Association for Supervision and Curriculum Development.

Tomlinson, C. A., (2001). *How to differentiate instruction in mixed-ability classrooms.* (2nd Ed.) Alexandria, VA: ASCD.

U.S. Census Bureau. American Fact Finder. (2008). *Florida: Selected Social Characteristics in the United States: 2006-2008 American Community Survey.* Retrieved May 8, 2010, from *http://factfinder.census.gov/servlet/ADPTable?_bm=y&-context=adp&-%20%20%20%20geo_id=04000US12&-qr_name=ACS_2008_3YR_G00_DP3YR2&-ds_name=ACS_2008_3YR_G00_&-tree_id=3308&-redoLog=false&-_caller=geoselect&-geo_id=04000US12&-format=&-_lang=en*

U.S. Department of Education. (2004, September). *The Elementary and Secondary Education Act as reauthorized by the No Child Left Behind Act of 2001; Part D-Enhancing education through technology, Sec. 2402.* Retrieved June 1, 2010, from http://www2.ed.gov/policy/elsec/leg/esea02/pg34.html

U.S. Department of Education (May 2, 2008). Title III of the Elementary and Secondary Education Act of 1965 (ESEA) as amended by the No Child Left Behind Act of 2001 (NCLB), *Federal Register, 73(86).* Retrieved June 2, 2010, from http://www2.ed.gov/legislation/FedRegister/other/2008-2/050208d.html

Vang, C. (2006). Minority parents should know more about school culture and its impact on their children's education. *Multicultural Education,* 14(1), 20-6.

THE LEARNING ENVIRONMENT

To maintain a student-centered learning environment that is safe, organized, equitable, flexible, inclusive, and collaborative, the effective educator consistently:

- Organizes, allocates, and manages the resources of time, space, and attention
- Manages individual and class behaviors through a well-planned management system
- Conveys high expectations to all students
- Respects students' cultural, linguistic and family background
- Models clear, acceptable oral and written communication skills
- Maintains a climate of openness, inquiry, fairness and support
- Integrates current information and communication technologies
- Adapts the learning environment to accommodate the differing needs and diversity of students
- Utilizes current and emerging assistive technologies that enable students to participate in high-quality communication interactions and achieve their educational goals.

Florida Educator Accomplished Practice #2:

THE LEARNING ENVIRONMENT

DID YOU KNOW…

Introduction:

An effective teacher establishes an environment that is not only conducive to learning but also a safe place to be. The learning environment covers the establishment of routines and rules, keeping the classroom running smoothly, arranging the physical environment of the room to facilitate learning, and implementing learning activities that help all students.

Vocabulary:

acceptable use policy (AUP) – a written agreement outlining the terms and conditions of Internet use

action zones – the areas in a classroom where a teacher directs most of his or her attention

affordances – opportunities offered a person by his or her environment

applied behavior analysis – the analysis of behavior problems and the prescription of remedies

assertive discipline – an approach to misbehavior based on principles of applied behavior analysis

assimilation – process of incorporating new experiences into existing concepts or cognitive structures

assistive technology – any service, item, or equipment used to maintain, improve, or increase the functional capabilities of students with disabilities

attention – the process of focusing on one aspect of the environment to the exclusion of other aspects

authoritative leadership – authority established through the flexible implementation of standards and characterized by discussion with and explanation to followers

CD-ROM (compact disc, read-only memory) – digitally encoded information permanently recorded on a compact disc (CD)

classroom management – actions taken by a teacher to facilitate student learning

cognitive development – changes in our capabilities as learners by which mental processes grow more complex and sophisticated

control theory – the view that students need to be empowered to control or meet their own needs and thus experience success in school

dangle – teacher starts an activity, stops it to turn to another, and never returns to the original activity

digital divide – the gap between people with access to technology and those with very limited or no access at all

discipline – the extent to which students are engaged in learning or other classroom-appropriate activities

distance learning – using the Internet to deliver instruction to students; also known as online learning, virtual learning, and e-learning

flash drive – a data storage device with a USB interface; a small device that is used to store and transfer information from a computer

flip-flop – the teacher starts an activity, stops it to turn to another, then returns to the original activity or drops it altogether

group fragmentation – teacher has students do something one at a time when the entire class could do the same thing collectively, results in reduction of the flow of class activities

I-message – a clear statement by a teacher that tells how he or she feels about misbehavior but does not lay blame on a student

instruction – the deliberate arrangement of learning conditions to promote the attainment of some intended goal

interactive whiteboard – (Promethean Board) oversized computer that can be used by the teacher to present what is on her/his desktop; an added feature is that students can respond to the teacher's questions and have it show up on the board

interjects irrelevancies – teacher is distracted by some unrelated event, object, or idea and reacts in such a way as to interrupt the on-going class activity

iPad – a device that is used solely for web browsing, watching movies, viewing photos, and emailing; known for its thin, vivid display and 9.7 inch screen

iPod – a digital music player used to download podcasts (a series of audio or video digital media files downloaded through web syndication)

LCD projector – a type of video projector for displaying video, images or computer data on a screen or other flat surface

learning-oriented classrooms – classrooms in which the teacher values learning and facilitates, rather than directs, student activity

low-key praise – praise given is almost unnoticeable by others

marker expression – teacher comment to students indicating that specific information is important to remember

marker technique – technique used by teacher to bring students' attention to specific information that is important to remember

misbehavior – any behavior by students that competes with or threatens learning activities

movement smoothness – teacher actions that allow smooth transitions from one activity to another or a smooth exchange of materials used in class

non-verbal communication – communication that does not involve speaking; can be by eye contact, smiling, or a tap on the desk

on-task behavior – any time a student is engaged with an academic task

overdwell – teacher engages in a series of actions or talk beyond what is necessary for students to understand the concept

overlapping – a teacher's ability to deal with more than one issue at the same time

physical knowledge – knowledge that one constructs about the environment through the use of the senses to perceive properties of objects

praise for compliance – teacher praises on-task students when another student is disruptive to influence the disruptive student to behave

procedures – standards of behavior that are specific to a particular classroom task or set of related tasks; routines

rules – general standards of behavior that have consequences; are meant to apply across all classroom situations

schemes – generalized ways of acting in the world, or modes of organization, that result in organizing objects or events into larger mental constructs

socio-arbitrary knowledge – culturally transmitted knowledge that is acquired through interaction with other people; includes language, moral rules, values, and systems of cultural symbols

specific praise – praise of appropriate behavior for a child who may frequently exhibit inappropriate behavior; should include particulars of the appropriate behavior and its value

task attraction – when introducing an assignment, the teacher uses words that will capture the interest of students

teacher power – the authority that teachers have available to them to manage student behavior; inversely, the extent to which students control their own behavior

verbal communication – communication by spoken word

withitness – the teacher's ability to observe all situations in the classroom and to deal effectively with student behavior

work-oriented classrooms – classrooms in which the teacher values production and student activity

Research

Classroom management is defined as the effort "to oversee the activities of the classroom, including learning, social interaction, and student behavior" (Martin, Yin & Baldwin, 1998). Teachers are expected to provide a safe and orderly environment in the classroom; when they are unable to do so, learning is affected. Not surprisingly, creating the best learning environment by using effective classroom management techniques is the primary focus for educators.

Three of the most well known classroom management models are Cooperative Discipline (Albert, 1989), Assertive Discipline (Canter & Canter, 2002), and CHAMPS (Sprick, 2009). A brief synopsis of each of these models appears below.

CLASSROOM MANAGEMENT MODELS

Cooperative Discipline (Linda Albert, 1989)

- The ultimate goal of student behavior is to "belong."
- Students misbehave to seek attention or power, to get revenge, or to avoid failure.

<u>Cooperative Discipline</u> Teachers:
- Make mistakes okay (remove the fear of mistakes)
- Build student confidence by using positive feedback
- Focus on students' past successes to build students' self-esteem
- Focus on the behavior, not the students
- Focus on the 5 "A's"—Acceptance, Attention, Appreciation, Affirmation and Affection

Assertive Discipline (Lee Canter, 1992)

- Teachers need to tell the students what they want from them.
- Teachers must give consequences if the students do not do what they are asked to do.
- Teachers should give students rewards for doing what is asked.

<u>Assertive Discipline</u> Teachers:
- Establish specific directions for each activity during the day and the exact behaviors they expect from the students
- Focus on students who do follow directions
- Do not administer a disciplinary consequence to a student until two students have been reinforced for behaving appropriately

- Use positive reinforcement and verbal praise
- Never argue with students

CHAMPS (Randy Sprick, 1998)

C = Conversation (Can students talk to each other during activity?)
H = Help (How do the students get the teacher's attention and get questions answered?)
A = Activity (What are the tasks and the objectives for the activity?)
M = Movement (Can students move about during this activity?)
P = Participation (What does the work behavior look and sound like?)

- Teachers should have a positive and proactive approach to classroom management.
- Teachers need to build positive relationships with students, communicating expectations during the first weeks of school.

CHAMPS Teachers:
- Have "bell work"
- Greet students as they enter class
- Have an "attention" signal
- Interact with students more often when the student is behaving
- Monitor student behavior by circulating and visually scanning
- Provide feedback during the activity and at the conclusion of the activity

WHAT YOU NEED TO KNOW...

The teacher has many roles in providing a supportive and flexible learning environment. These roles include managing the classroom, providing for student safety, fostering respect for students' cultural and family backgrounds, and acting as an advocate for students. Other roles may include preparing bulletin boards, escorting students to the cafeteria, and supervising detention hall, bus duty, and hall duty.

MANAGEMENT OF STUDENT CONDUCT

Effective teachers explain and monitor class rules and procedures, are aware of everything occurring in the classroom ("withitness"), have smooth transitions between activities, and use praise to encourage appropriate behavior.

Seating Chart

Effective teachers set up a seating chart for the first day of school. Seating charts can easily be changed after a couple of weeks to handle any problems that have arisen. Seating charts are important because they:
- facilitate taking of attendance while students are doing independent work,
- help teachers learn the names of students, and
- assist substitutes when the teacher is absent.

Bell Work

Getting students to work as soon as they enter the classroom can be challenging. Effective teachers use bell work, which are activities that keep students busy as soon as class begins. Bell work, written in a designated area on the board, can be reviews or an introduction to the day's lesson. This is the "quiet" time teachers should use to take class attendance.

Examples of Bell Work

Elementary: Write complete sentences for each of the following words:
decide, identify, predict

Secondary: If you could visit any country we studied this week, which country would you visit? Why?

Class Rules

A rule is a standard of behavior that involves a consequence if the rule is broken. Effective teachers explain and monitor their class rules and enforce them immediately and consistently. Teachers should never create more than five rules because more than five rules are difficult for students to remember. Students, parents and school administrators should all receive copies of the classroom rules. Always have students practice the rules (or have a student demonstrate the rules) when they are presented to the class.

> **Example**: "Three tardies to class will result in a 30-minute detention." *(The detention is the consequence.)*
>
> **Non-Example**: "Sharpen your pencil before class begins." *(This is a procedure.)*

Procedures

A procedure involves student behavior that helps the classroom run efficiently. Procedures, which eventually become routines, do not involve any disciplinary consequences if the students do not follow them.

> **Example**: Students place their homework on a table when they enter class.
>
> **Non-Example**: Teacher tells students if they continue to talk she will call their parents.

Withitness

An effective teacher is aware of everything going on in the classroom. This includes stopping misbehavior before it spreads, handling more than one disruption at a time, correctly identifying the student who is misbehaving, and correcting misbehavior while presenting a lesson.

When a student is misbehaving, the teacher needs to make eye contact with the student, explain what the student is doing wrong, and redirect the student to the task. At all times, the teacher needs to treat the student with respect and avoid yelling. While presenting a lesson, the teacher can redirect misbehavior by moving near the misbehaving student and lightly tapping on the student's desk.

Loudly calling out the name of a misbehaving student while teaching a lesson may only result in distracting all the students in class and getting them off task. It may also embarrass or challenge the student and result in more misbehavior. It is best to talk to the student in isolation and find out the cause for the disruption.

Smooth Transitions

Effective teachers make smooth transitions between activities, do not react to irrelevant questions or comments by students, do not overdwell, and do not flip-flop between instructional content.

Everyone knows that students will talk or misbehave when teachers are busy with their own tasks and not paying attention to the class. For that reason, teachers must plan well, have all materials on hand, and move quickly from one activity to the next.

Some students enjoy asking questions that have nothing to do with the lesson. Younger children may want to share a story they feel is related to the topic being discussed. Unless the teacher asks for an example for reinforcement of a concept, it is best to ask them to share their story at recess. If the teacher lets one student share without it being part of the lesson plan, other students see this as an opportunity to share their stories. Older students may ask questions solely for the purpose of distracting the teacher and getting off task. Although some teachers just ignore these questions, others tell the students to stay after class at which time the question will be addressed. Not surprisingly, most of the students do not remain after class.

At times, teachers are at fault for getting their students off task. Teachers who overdwell on the material or flip-flop between topics can be responsible for students losing focus.

Praise

Praise can be a useful tool for managing the learning environment. Teachers need to remember that praise needs to be specific, focusing on the behavior and not the student. For example, a teacher notices that Patricia constantly fools around when the class lines up to go to the playground. One day, noting that Patricia is standing appropriately in line, the teacher praises her for her conduct and points out that the class will be able to get to the playground earlier.

Angry Students

Sometimes a student has difficulty controlling angry feelings. When this occurs, a teacher should not ignore the inappropriate behavior. Depending on the situation, the teacher can:

- respond to the student in a quiet manner,
- speak privately with the student to determine the cause for the anger,
- remind the student of choices and consequences,
- encourage the student by recognizing the student's strengths, and/or
- refer the student to a counselor to learn strategies for controlling anger.

Bullying

The Florida Department of Education defines bullying as any "unwanted and repeated written, verbal, or physical behavior, including any threatening, insulting, or dehumanizing gesture, by an adult or student that is severe or pervasive enough to create an intimidating, hostile or offensive educational environment, cause discomfort or humiliation, or unreasonably interfere with the individual's school performance or participation" (Florida Department of Education, 2008).

Bullying may involve unwanted teasing, threats, intimidation, stalking, cyber stalking, cyber bullying, physical violence, harassment, and public humiliation. Studies of bullying in schools indicate the following:
- Bullying takes place more often in the school than on the way to and from the school (Sampson, 2009).
- Approximately 20.5% of elementary schools, 43.5% of middle schools and 21.7% of high schools reported incidents of bullying occurring at least once a week during the 2007-08 school year (National Center for Education Statistics, 2010).
- Approximately 32% of students ages 12-18 have reported being bullied at school or cyber-bullied during the school day (National Center for Education Statistics, 2010).

Teachers need to be aware of bullying behavior since studies indicate most students do not report bullying to adults. Whereas boy bullies tend to rely on physical and verbal aggression, girls are more likely to bully through rumor-spreading, teasing, and social isolation. The reasons victims give for not telling teachers include fear of retaliation, feeling shame, not wanting to worry their parents, and having no confidence the teacher could improve the situation (Sampson, 2009).

CLASSROOM PHYSICAL ENVIRONMENT

Space

Personal teaching style and specific educational needs determine how a teacher sets up a classroom. Teachers who use collaborative activities might organize tables or desks in clusters. For whole group instruction, teachers might feel more comfortable using a U-shaped seating arrangement; while teachers who give out independent work might feel more comfortable with the traditional single row of desks. Whichever seating arrangements are created, teachers need to be sure the seating accommodates students with special needs.

Supplies and equipment need to be easily accessible to eliminate disruptions and time delays. Materials frequently used by students, such as paste, markers and paper, need to be available in several areas of a room.

Environment

The temperature of the classroom, lighting, and outside noise level are three important facets of the learning environment. Although teachers may not be able to control the temperature of the classroom, lighting and noise level need to be addressed since they can affect student performance.

Bulletin boards reflect what the teacher feels is important. They should be used to reinforce instructional goals, communicate essential information, motivate students, and make the classroom a more appealing place to learn.

The classroom always needs to be clean. Students should be instructed to pick up trash and dispose of it in waste containers. Before students leave a classroom, they need to return materials to the storage area; desks/tables should be placed in their original location.

Teachers should take every opportunity to familiarize themselves with the policies and rules of their school and district. Some of the most important rules, regulations, and policies include:
- supervision of students before school, during school, after school, and on field trips;
- out-of-classroom policies for students going to other areas of the school;
- dismissal procedures from the class; and
- emergency dismissal procedures, including fire drills, tornado drills, and emergency evacuations.

TEACHER BEHAVIORS & THE CLASSROOM ENVIRONMENT

In *Setting Limits in the Classroom*, Mackenzie and Stanzione (2010) identified four types of teacher behavior that affect a classroom's environment: Permissive Approach, Punitive Approach, Mixed Approach, and Democratic Approach.

- Permissive Approach ("Respectful but Not Firm")
  The teacher who uses this approach in the classroom spends a lot of time warning and offering second chances, gives unclear directions, and begs students to cooperate. If consequences are given, they are usually ineffective. Students learn the teacher rarely follows through and continue to misbehave.

- Punitive Approach ("Firm but Not Respectful")
  The teacher who uses this approach in the classroom intimidates, threatens, and shames students. Severe penalties are handed out for misbehavior. Students become resentful, often retaliate, and may engage in power struggles with the teacher.

- Mixed Approach ("Neither Firm nor Respectful")
  The teacher who uses this approach in the classroom is inconsistent. One minute the teacher is permissive, giving students additional chances. When that does not work, the teacher becomes frustrated and reverts to threatening and shaming the students. As long as the teacher is inconsistent, students continue to misbehave. They do not take the teacher seriously until the teacher begins to threaten them.

- Democratic Approach ("Firm and Respectful")
  The teacher who uses this approach in the classroom is respectful towards students, explains rules and procedures, and is fair and consistent when holding students accountable for their actions. Students take responsibility for their behavior and learn self-control.

Effective teachers use the Democratic Approach. When students know what is expected of them in the classroom, the teacher is able to spend more time teaching and less time correcting misbehavior.

TOP TEN INSTRUCTIONAL ORGANIZATION AND DEVELOPMENT TIPS FOR EFFECTIVE CLASSROOM MANAGEMENT

1. Establish rapport and learn the students' names quickly.

2. Arrange the classroom and student seating to meet instructional goals.

3. Begin instruction promptly and conduct beginning/ending reviews.

4. Orient students to the content being presented and maintain academic focus throughout the class session.

5. Handle materials in an organized manner.

6. Ask lower and higher order questions throughout the lesson to check for comprehension and to enhance critical thinking. Engage students in the learning process!

7. Recognize student responses by amplifying, probing, repeating, rephrasing, and giving corrective feedback. Use specific praise when appropriate.

8. Provide for practice to support mastery of content/skills.

9. Give clear, concise directions for seatwork and homework. Always check for comprehension. Give specific concrete feedback on all assignments.

10. Circulate and assist students during seatwork.

REPORTING CHILD MALTREATMENT: CHILD ABUSE

The classroom teacher has the most contact and interaction with students. Observations about student achievement, attendance, home life, illness, and needs come from classroom teachers. For this reason, teachers are required by law to report suspected child abuse.

Mandatory Reporting of Child Maltreatment

Florida Statute 415.504 requires teachers to report suspected child abuse. The law clearly states that mandated reporting applies to any child, not just the children with which teachers work.

When, Where and How to Report

Child maltreatment should be reported as soon as the teacher is aware or suspects abuse or neglect is occurring. Failure to report is considered a misdemeanor of the first degree. Conviction includes imprisonment of up to one year and/or a fine of up to $1,000 (Florida Statute 39.205 (1)). Child maltreatment should be reported to the Florida Abuse Registry: 1-800-96-ABUSE.

Confidentiality

School teachers are required to give their names to the abuse hotline staff (Florida Statute 39.201 (1) (b)). Although the names of the reporters will be entered on the report, the names will be considered confidential.

Notice of Completion: Reporters of child maltreatment may request, at the time of the report, that the DCF notify them of the completion of the child protective investigation.

PHYSICAL AND BEHAVIORAL INDICATORS OF CHILD ABUSE & NEGLECT

TYPE OF ABUSE	PHYSICAL INDICATORS	BEHAVIORAL INDICATORS
PHYSICAL ABUSE	Unexplained bruises and welts on body • May be in various stages of healing • Regularly appear after student's absences, vacations or weekends Unexplained fractures • Multiple fractures • Various stages of healing Unexplained abrasions or lacerations • Appear on mouth, lips, gums, eyes, external genital area	Wary of adults Behavioral Extremes • Aggressiveness • Withdrawal • Overly compliant Afraid to go home Complains of soreness and moves awkwardly Avoids physical contact or touch Wears clothing that covers the body Early to school; stays late as if afraid to go home
PHYSICAL NEGLECT	Consistent hunger, poor hygiene, inappropriate clothing Unattended physical problems or medical needs Abandonment Distended stomach, emaciated	Begging or stealing food Constant fatigue or falling asleep States there is no adult at home Frequent school absences or tardiness Destructive
SEXUAL ABUSE	Difficulty in walking or sitting Torn, stained or bloody underwear Pain or itching in genital area Bruises or bleeding in anal, genital, or vaginal areas Venereal disease Frequent urinary or yeast infections	Unwilling to participate in certain physical activities Sudden drop in school grades Withdrawal, fantasy, or unusually infantile behavior Crying without reason; suicide attempts Sexually provocative Chronic runaway
EMOTIONAL ABUSE	Speech disorder Lags in physical development Substance abuse	Sucking thumb, biting, rocking Antisocial or destructive Behavioral extremes—inappropriate (infantile or adult) Lags in mental or emotional development

LEARNING ENVIRONMENT AND
THEORIES OF LEARNING

Experienced teachers acknowledge that no two classes are alike. Although all children of a certain age have some things in common, all classes and all children are different. Effective teachers understand how children learn, show respect for their diverse talents, and provide appropriate learning environments. They must frequently assess the students' understanding of the content and the appropriateness of the instructional strategies used.

Learning theories describe the complex process of how students learn. The major educational learning theories are Behaviorism, Cognitivism, Constructivism, and Humanism.

Behaviorism

Behaviorism regards the student as a passive learner who begins as a clean slate. Learning is shaped by repetition and reinforcement (positive or negative) as the student responds to stimuli provided by the teacher.

> *Classroom Use*: lectures, copying notes, learning by rote, and watching demonstrations

Cognitivism

According to Cognitivism, learning is a process of relating new knowledge to previously learned information. In this theory, learning takes place when students can process, organize, and retrieve information as needed. Learning focuses on thinking, memory, and problem solving. The role of the teacher is to guide and provide an educational environment in which students can explore and reflect.

> *Classroom Use:* case studies, research, discussions, presentations, and self-assessment

Constructivism

Constructivists believe learning is an active process in which students should learn to discover facts, concepts, and principles for themselves. The teacher is considered to be a facilitator who provides guidelines and creates the environment for students to draw their own conclusions.

Jerome Bruner often is credited for originating Discovery Learning, a constructivist-based approach to education, in the 1960s. Discovery Learning has students using their own past experiences to discover facts and relationships.

Classroom Use: experimentation, project based learning, research projects, field trips, and videos (all followed by class discussions)

Humanism

Humanists believe learning should be student centered and personalized. Students explore, observe, and take responsibility for their own learning. The teacher is a role model, teaches general learning skills, encourages group work, provides a supportive environment, and serves as a facilitator in the classroom.

Classroom Use: cooperative learning, games, simulations, role-playing, and activities involving exploration and student interaction

HIGH EXPECTATIONS & THE LEARNING ENVIRONMENT

Research has shown that effective teachers communicate high expectations to all students and behave in a manner that is consistent with those expectations. This is achieved through the affective tone of the teacher and the quality of student-teacher interactions (Marzano, 2007).

Good teachers know that students will succeed if they receive support and encouragement. They tell their students they expect them to achieve, they interact with low- and high-achieving students, and they explain the relationship between effort and achievement. The messages given are (Cross, 2008):
- "The content and skills being taught in this class are important."
- "You have the ability to learn the course content."
- "I am not going to let you fail because I know you can do it."

Effective teachers know how to praise, when to praise, and how to criticize constructively. Students soon realize they are respected and valued by their teachers, and begin to put forth more effort and behave accordingly.

STUDENT MOTIVATION

Every teacher knows that motivating students to learn and behave is the key to success. Some students enter the classroom already highly motivated. They are alert, focused, and authentically engaged in the learning process. However, other students are not self-motivated. They are easily distracted, bored, appear to be lazy, and resist the teacher's best efforts to engage them in the lesson.

Behaviors & Student Motivation

According to researchers, there are five patterns of behavior that explain student motivation (Seifert, 2004). These patterns are:

1. Strong Sense of Self: Students with a *Strong Sense of Self* are confident they can do the work presented by the teacher. They are willing to face challenging and difficult problems. They come to class ready to learn and present few behavior problems.

2. Failure Avoidance: Students driven by *Failure Avoidance* make negative self-statements. They believe they cannot control outcomes so they adopt failure-avoiding behaviors to protect their self-worth. If students are having problems learning concepts, they may misbehave in class. They would rather be sent to the office on a discipline referral than be labeled a "failure" by fellow classmates of the teacher.

3. <u>Learned Helplessness</u>: Students characterized with *Learned Helplessness* believe any effort they make in class is useless. They see the tasks they do in class as always ending in failure. If they do have success, they will not take credit for it; they regard their success as "luck." They experience boredom, humiliation, and shame. Teachers often get upset at these students because they do not appear to put forth any effort when doing classwork.

4. <u>Work Avoidant</u>: Students who are *Work Avoidant* are bright but bored. They believe the work they do has little meaning and will only do enough work to get by.

5. <u>Hostile Work-Avoidant</u>: Students who are *Hostile Work-Avoidant* can also be considered passive-aggressive. For some reason, they are angry with the teacher and refuse to do work. In their minds, their lack of work is an attempt to seek revenge on the teacher.

Motivating Students

Effective teachers can motivate students by:
- having good lesson plans that keep students engaged,
- writing positive comments when grading student work,
- posting student work on the bulletin board for other students to see,
- recognizing good responses to questions asked in class, and
- identifying topics that interest their students.

TECHNOLOGY & THE LEARNING ENVIRONMENT

The No Child Left Behind Act sets three goals for technology in education: (1) improve student achievement with the use of technology, (2) ensure every student is technologically literate by the time the student completes the eighth grade, and (3) encourage effective integration of technology with teacher staff development and curriculum development (U.S. Department of Education, 2004).

All teachers need to be techno-savvy. They should be able to operate a computer and printer; use word processing, presentation and spreadsheet applications; use search engines; and communicate through email. The digital age has revolutionized their roles. Lesson plans can be accessed and downloaded from web sites. Computers, DVDs, digital scanners, LCD projectors, interactive white boards, flash drives, smart phones, iPads and iPods are just a few of the technological tools available. Although schools may differ as to the type of technology accessible to teachers and students, teachers should utilize the resources as much as possible when creating lessons.

Teachers also need to give students more active roles in their own learning by providing them opportunities to use technology in the classroom. They should be aware, however, of web sites accessed by their students. Firewall software can be utilized to restrict student access to sites that are inappropriate.

USING TECHNOLOGY IN THE CLASSROOM

Teachers need to consider several items when utilizing technology in the classroom (Kingsley, 2007). These include:

- receiving appropriate training and staying abreast of current and new technology;
- using digital tools appropriate for the lesson and evaluating their effectiveness;
- understanding the school district's Acceptable Use Policy for the Internet;
- following copyright and fair use policies;
- understanding online safety and etiquette;
- addressing content and technology standards in lessons;
- collaborating with other teachers;
- identifying and bookmarking useful Web sites; and
- using technology to differentiate instruction.

The integration of technology into lessons makes the classroom seem more like the real world to students. With technology, students are no longer limited by the resources available in their textbooks, school, or community. They become engaged learners who can collaborate with their peers.

Technology has several roles in the classroom. Computers and iPods can be used as tutors, teaching a skill and then drilling the student until the skill is learned. Computer applications can be used by students to search for information, perform calculations, and create multi-media presentations and documents. When considering the integration of technology into lessons, teachers should ask the following questions:

- What do I want to teach?
- Will technology enhance the lesson and students' learning?
- Will the technology appeal to all ability levels and learning styles?
- Will students work independently or in collaborative groups?
- What type of technology is available?
- What applications are available?
- Do students have the basic skills necessary to use the technology?
- What technological support is available?
- What can be done if the technology fails?
- Will students have access to the technology in their homes?

Research has shown that using technology can have an effect on classrooms and students. When students use technology, they:

- become active rather than passive learners;
- make choices on how to obtain, manipulate, and display information;
- become more motivated and self-esteem rises;
- are more able to handle complex assignments;
- are more inclined to work cooperatively and provide peer tutoring; and
- use more outside resources.

When teachers use technology, they become *facilitators* of knowledge, instead of *dispensers of information*.

ASSISTIVE TECHNOLOGY IN THE CLASSROOM

The 1997 amendments to the Individuals with Disabilities Education Act require assistive technology be considered for every student receiving special education services. These devices are used to maintain, improve, or increase the functional capabilities of students with disabilities. Some examples are:
- speech recognition system – enables students to control computers by simply speaking
- personal reading machine – machine scans printed pages and immediately "reads" the pages out loud
- video captioning devices – enables hearing impaired to read spoken dialogue on a video
- large print/screen magnification hardware and software – helps visually impaired students read printed material
- Braille writer – enables vision impaired students to take notes
- Braille translation software – translates text into Braille for vision impaired students

- communication boards – helps students who have difficulty in communicating effectively by using pictures and symbols
- talking calculators – helps students by reciting numbers, symbols, or functions when keys are pressed
- voice-to-text or text-to-voice software – helps students communicate
- foot pedal or switch – used as an alternative device for students who cannot operate a computer mouse

Distance Learning

Distance learning, using technology instead of the traditional classroom setting, emerged as a response to the problem of providing access to education for those who could not participate in face-to-face classes. The benefits of distance education include (Watson, 2007):
- providing opportunities for students unable to attend traditional schools;
- providing highly qualified teachers in subjects where qualified teachers are lacking;
- expanding the courses available to students (beyond what a single school can offer);
- providing course flexibility to students facing scheduling conflicts; and
- affording opportunities for at-risk students, elite athletes and performers, dropouts, migrant youth, incarcerated or pregnant students, and students who are homebound due to illness or injury; allowing them to continue their studies outside the classroom.

Disadvantages of distance learning include (Cavanaugh, et.al, 2004; Watson 2007):
- student isolation,
- lack of student social development,
- the inability of students to demonstrate physical skills,
- academic dishonesty, and
- authenticity of student work.

Role of the Teacher in Distance Learning:

The distance-learning teacher has several roles. These roles include:
- developing the online course content,
- identifying the method of instructional delivery,
- identifying methods for communicating with the students (email, telephone, chat room),
- guiding and individualizing learning, and
- identifying methods to assess student progress.

When used appropriately, distance learning "can improve how students learn, can improve what students learn, and can deliver high-quality learning opportunities to *all* children" (National Association of State Boards of Education, 2001, p. 4).

Virtual Schools

Virtual schools are online learning opportunities that provide students with access to age- and ability-appropriate curriculum. Statewide virtual schools exist in 27 states, while other states offer full-time online schools to only some of their students. Legislation in 2008 and 2009 required all Florida school districts to offer full-time online programs for grades K-12. Today, The Florida Virtual Schools is the largest virtual school in the United States (Watson, et.al, 2009).

TEACHER COMMUNICATION & THE LEARNING ENVIRONMENT

Do you say what you mean? Command of verbal and non-verbal language in the classroom plays an important role in determining the teacher's effectiveness. Teachers must remember to model clear and acceptable communication skills at all times.

Control Discourse — Make a point quickly and avoid vague words such as "some," "about," "that guy," "something," etc.

Non-Example: "That *country* attacked an *island prior* to the *war*."
Example: "Japan attacked Pearl Harbor, Hawaii, on December 7, 1941."

Use Markers — Use markers to emphasize what is important for students to remember. These markers can be expressions, techniques, or repetition. See the examples below.

Marker Expressions: "This is important to remember."   "You will be seeing this again on a test."
Marker Techniques: Teacher <u>underlines</u> a word or phrase on the board or in a prepared technology presentation.   Teacher uses different colors for work on the board or in a prepared technology presentation.

Use Repetition — When introducing new material, teachers need to repeat the information a minimum of three times in spaced intervals. The repetition should be during the lesson, at least once during the week, and at a later time.

Express Verbal Enthusiasm — Present course content with enthusiasm to catch the interest of students.

Non-Example: "I know some people don't like Shakespeare but we have to read this play."
Example: "Today we are going to read a great love story about two teenagers, *Romeo and Juliet.* You are really going to love this play by Shakespeare."

Use Task Attraction — When introducing an assignment, use words that will capture your students' interest.

Non-Example: "You have to do a three-page report on Australia."
Example: "Instead of writing a report, you are going to use your research to create a travel brochure on Australia."

Challenge Students — When introducing a difficult assignment, let the students know they are capable of producing outstanding work.

Non-Example: "This is going to be a difficult assignment but you have to do it."
Example: "This is going to be a difficult assignment but this class is capable of doing great work. I know you have always met the challenges in the past and I anticipate this time will be the same."

Use Appropriate Body Language—Body language is an essential component of communication in the classroom. Non-verbal messages can make a difference to students and how they learn. Teachers need to:

Smile Frequently	• Conveys friendliness and affiliation with the students
Nod Encouragement	• Conveys positive reinforcement • Indicates teacher is listening to the student
Make Frequent Eye Contact	• Conveys interest in the student • Conveys warmth
Gesture While Speaking	• Captures students' attention • Facilitates learning

Use Humor — Humor can eliminate stress or tension, but must not be used to humiliate or embarrass students. Teachers should not use sarcasm.

Although students are different from each other, they share common characteristics at specific grade levels. Teachers should consider these characteristics when establishing the learning environment for their classrooms (Kelly, 1989; Pennington, 2008; Pennington, 2009).

Kindergarten – 5 Year Olds
- Can combine simple ideas into complex relationships
- Need printed materials that stimulate the development of literacy and language skills
- Need variety of experiences to develop cognitive, physical, emotional and social skills

Students in the Classroom:
- need items to play with and manipulate,
- crave attention and praise,
- get frustrated with serious people and serious talk, and
- get along with members of the opposite sex

First Grade – 6 Year Olds
- Active learners
- Demonstrate considerable verbal skills
- Love games and rules that help them to develop concept and problem-solving skills
- Enjoy hands-on activities and experimentation

Students in the Classroom:
- cannot stay still,
- find it difficult finishing what they start,
- find it difficult copying from the board,
- love their teacher by the end of the year,
- enjoy interaction with others, and
- differ in their physical abilities. (Boys usually use their legs and arms better than girls do; girls usually use their eyes and hands better than boys do.)

Second Grade – 7 Year Olds
- Able to reason, listen to others, and demonstrate social give-and-take
- Flexible, open-minded, and tolerant of unfamiliar ideas

Students in the Classroom:
- are changing (Not only are their bodies changing, their personalities are becoming more distinct.),

o should be encouraged to accept their differences (handprints, family photographs, favorite clothes, etc.),
o can only concentrate on a subject for 20 minutes, and
o enjoy repetition. (They should only move on to the next lesson when the last one has been mastered.)

Third Grade – 8 Year Olds
- Combine curiosity with social interest
- Comprehension of ideas is dependent upon relating ideas to their own experiences

Students in the Classroom:
o like school but are very casual about it,
o are talkative in the lunchroom and on the playground to those they like,
o need to inspect, know, organize, and classify, and
o have a wide range of abilities in reading and math.

Fourth Grade – 9 Year Olds
- Are self-conscious
- Prefer group activities to working alone
- Understand abstractions and cause-and-effect relationships
- Need real experiences in social settings

Students in the Classroom:
o have become individuals and want everyone to know it,
o consider friends to be more important than the teacher,
o begin to think of "school" as more real,
o are more absorbed and competitive,
o want to improve upon their past accomplishments,
o are more competitive so cheating can become a problem, and
o divide themselves according to gender. (Girls walk together and boys fool around together.)

Fifth Grade – 10 Year Olds
- Are experiencing bodily changes and growth spurts
- May experience periods of frustration and anger
- Are interested about places and problems in the news

Students in the Classroom:
o are growing mentally and physically,
o are on the verge of abstract thought,
o consider school more demanding,
o consider honor and fair play to be important,

o consider friends to be more important than teachers and parents, and
o usually have friendships with the same sex, but boy-girl flirtation does take place.

Sixth to Eighth Grade – 11 to 13 Year Olds

- Curious
- Willing to learn things they consider useful
- Enjoy solving "real-life" problems
- Focused on themselves and how their peers perceive them
- Beginning to assert independence and resist adult authority
- Beginning to think critically

Students in the Classroom:
o need to be a part of a peer group consisting of boys and girls,
o are influenced by peer pressure,
o prefer to work with their peers,
o need frequent physical activity and movement, and
o need adult support and direction.

Ninth to Twelfth Grade – 14 to 17 Year Olds

- Need to understand the purpose of instructional activities they are given
- Are internally and externally motivated
- May have cognitive barriers due to academic failure or lack of self-confidence
- Want to assume own responsibility for learning
- Can think abstractly

Students in the Classroom:
o are interested in co-educational activities,
o want to make their own plans (with adults assuming a supportive role),
o are developing a community consciousness, and
o need opportunities for expressing themselves.

SEVEN CORRELATES OF EFFECTIVE SCHOOLS

In 1991, Lawrence Lezotte (Lezotte,1991) identified seven areas that all effective schools have in common. In all of these correlates, the teacher and the learning environment play important roles. The correlates are:

1. Safe and Orderly Environment—Students and staff feel safe on the campus; emphasis is placed on presence of desirable behaviors for learning.
2. Climate of High Expectations for Success—Teachers and administrators have high expectations of all their students; teachers will use appropriate strategies to assure all students reach mastery.
3. Instructional Leadership—Administrators and teacher leaders all are working to improve student achievement.
4. Clear and Focused Mission—Faculty, staff, parents, and members of the community understand the school's mission; there will be balance between low and higher levels of learning.
5. Opportunity to Learn and Student Time on Task—All students are given the opportunity to learn and students are always on task; teachers will need to become more skilled at interdisciplinary teaching.
6. Frequent Monitoring of Student Progress—There are frequent assessment and re-assessment of student progress; authentic assessments will be emphasized; technology will assist teachers and students in the monitoring of student progress.
7. Home-School Relationships—Parents frequently attend school meetings and activities; good communication and trust exist between the school and the parents; teachers and parents work together to meet the needs of the students.

LET IT SHOW!

Below is a list of different methods you can use to demonstrate your accomplishment of **FEAP #2: THE LEARNING ENVIRONMENT**.

(a) Organizes, allocates, and manages the resources of time, space, and attention
- ▶ <u>Create classroom-seating arrangements to meet instructional needs</u>.
- ▶ <u>Create a classroom management plan:</u> Create procedures for everyday tasks to keep the classroom running smoothly, such as handing in assignments, sharpening pencils, bathroom breaks, arrival, dismissal, movement within the classroom, etc.
- ▶ <u>Create a Discovery Center</u>: Create an area in your classroom where students can explore, manipulate objects, and solve problems.

(b) Manages individual and class behaviors through a well-planned management system
- ▶ <u>Create a Behavior Management Plan</u>: Create a behavior management plan that includes rules, consequences, and positive reinforcement techniques.
- ▶ <u>Create a Cafeteria Plan</u>: Create a plan for your elementary students when they are in the cafeteria.
- ▶ <u>Create Playground Rules</u>: Demonstrate your ability to develop a safety plan to protect students from being harmed on the school's playground.
- ▶ <u>Develop Conflict Resolution Lessons</u>: Demonstrate your ability to assist students in resolving conflicts in a manner that does not expose them to embarrassment or disparagement.

(c) Conveys high expectations to all students
- ▶ <u>Develop a Reward Program</u>: Develop a reward system for students with improved behavior.
- ▶ <u>Create Learning Activities</u>: Demonstrate your knowledge of learning theories by creating instructional activities that engage all of your students in the learning process.
- ▶ <u>Create an Academic Improvement Plan</u>: Identify the instructional needs of one of your students. Create an Academic Improvement Plan for the student using strategies that meet the student's learning style.
- ▶ <u>Send a Letter Home</u>: Send a translated letter home to parents of non-English speaking students. The letter should contain information about the curriculum, behavior expectations, grading, and how they can help their student.
- ▶ <u>Use a Challenging Statement</u>: Demonstrate your ability to create high expectations by introducing a difficult assignment with a challenging statement.

(d) Respects students' cultural, linguistic and family background
- ▶ <u>Create a Multicultural Lesson</u>: Create a lesson that highlights the contributions of other cultures.
- ▶ <u>Create a Lesson Plan Based on Multicultural Mandates</u>: Create a lesson plan based on one of Florida's Multicultural Mandates—History of the Holocaust; contributions of African-Americans, Hispanics, or women; or Character Education.
- ▶ <u>Develop a world cultural exchange day</u> and invite families to participate.

(e) Models clear, acceptable oral and written communication skills
- ▶ <u>Keep a file</u> of all correspondence to students, parents and administrators demonstrating your ability.
- ▶ <u>Video tape a lesson</u>.
- ▶ <u>Create a Kindness Chart</u>: Develop a Kindness chart to recognize students who have demonstrated kindness toward others. Explain to your students the meaning of "kindness" and model behaviors that demonstrate the character trait.

(f) Maintains a climate of openness, inquiry, fairness and support
- ▶ <u>Using a world map, create a visual representation of your class</u> (use information such as where they were born, cultural heritage, etc.).
- ▶ <u>Create a Bulletin Board</u>: Create a bulletin board that will improve the learning environment in your classroom.
- ▶ <u>Attend a Child Abuse Workshop</u>: Demonstrate your knowledge of the Child Abuse Law and the legal obligation of teachers to protect the health and safety of their students.
- ▶ <u>Learn About Child Abuse</u>: Attend a Child Abuse workshop offered by your school district. Reflect on what you learned.

(g) Integrates current information and communication technologies
- ▶ <u>Create a Lesson</u>: Create a lesson that requires your use of technology.
- ▶ <u>Use Technology</u>: Use presentation software (PowerPoint) to teach a lesson.
- ▶ <u>Use Technology</u>: Have students create software presentations or videos to showcase their creativity and critical thinking skills.
- ▶ <u>Virtual Field Trip</u>: Create a lesson in which your students can take a virtual field trip.
- ▶ <u>Use a Video</u>: Incorporate a video into a lesson
- ▶ <u>Project based learning</u>: Have students produce a project utilizing searches conducted on their smart phones or computers.

(h) Adapts the learning environment to accommodate the differing needs and diversity of students

▶ Create a Seating Chart: Create a seating chart with special adaptations for any LEP, Hearing Impaired, Sight Impaired, or Physically Handicapped students in your class.

(i) Utilizes current and emerging assistive technologies that enable students to participate in high-quality communication interactions and achieve their educational goals

▶ Using Assistive Technology: Identify a special needs student in your class who could benefit from the use of assistive technology. Meet with appropriate staff members to arrange for the installation of the technology in your classroom.

ACTIVITY OVERVIEW FOR DEMONSTRATING PROFICIENCY IN
FEAP #2: THE LEARNING ENVIRONMENT

(a) Organizes, allocates, and manages the resources of time, space, and attention

Activity B: SEATING ARRANGEMENTS & INSTRUCTIONAL STRATEGIES

(b) Manages individual and class behaviors through a well-planned management system

Activity C: CREATING RULES & PROCEDURES

(c) Conveys high expectations to all students

Activity A: THEORIES OF LEARNING ACTIVITIES

(d) Respects students' cultural, linguistic and family background

Activity D: STUDENT NEEDS & INSTRUCTIONAL DECISIONS

(e) Models clear, acceptable oral and written communication skills

Activity C: CREATING RULES & PROCEDURES

(f) Maintains a climate of openness, inquiry, fairness and support

Activity C: CREATING RULES & PROCEDURES

(g) Integrates current information and communication technologies

Activity F: INTEGRATION OF TECHNOLOGY

(h) Adapts the learning environment to accommodate the differing needs and diversity of students

Activity D: STUDENT NEEDS & INSTRUCTIONAL DECISIONS
Activity E: LEP JOURNAL ABSTRACT

(i) Utilizes current and emerging assistive technologies that enable students to participate in high-quality communication interactions and achieve their educational goals

Activity F: INTEGRATION OF TECHNOLOGY

ACTIVITY A

THEORIES OF LEARNING ACTIVITIES (FEAP 2)

The purpose of this activity is to create two activities that show a relationship to a learning theory and create a climate of student inquiry.

1. Identify the specific learning theory for which you will be creating two instructional activities. (Behaviorism, Cognitivism, Constructivism, Humanism, Multiple Intelligences, Discovery Learning)

   _____

2. Give a brief overview of the theory.

   _____

   _____

   _____

Activity # 1

Subject area _____ Grade _____

Name of activity: _____

Describe the activity you have chosen or developed and discuss specifically how you will implement it in your specific subject area.

List materials needed by the student and the teacher.

Explain how this activity encourages inquiry.

Explain how this activity is related to the learning theory you selected.

Activity # 2

Subject area _____ Grade _____

Name of activity: _____

Describe the activity you have chosen or developed and discuss specifically how you will implement it in your specific subject area.

List materials needed by the student and the teacher.

Explain how this activity encourages inquiry.

Explain how this activity is related to the learning theory you selected.

ACTIVITY B

SEATING ARRANGEMENTS & INSTRUCTIONAL STRATEGIES (FEAP 2)

Directions: Review the four seating arrangements in this activity. First, identify the advantages and disadvantages for the teacher and the students. Then, identify the instructional strategies and activities that would be most effective for each seating arrangement.

SPLIT

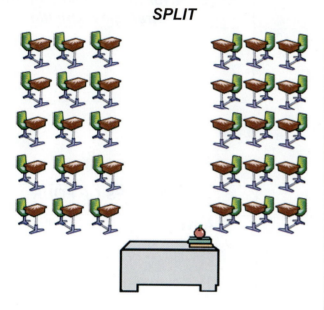

SPLIT	
Advantage	**Disadvantage**
Effective for the following instructional strategies/activities	

U-SHAPED

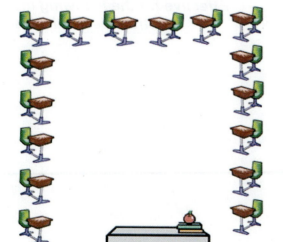

U-SHAPED	
Advantage	**Disadvantage**
Effective for the following instructional strategies/activities	

V-ROUND TABLES

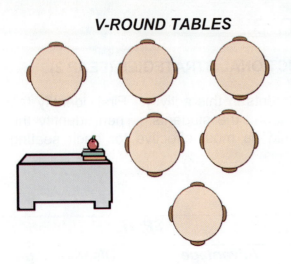

V-ROUND TABLES	
Advantage	**Disadvantage**
Effective for the following instructiona *strategies/activities*	

TABLES OF FOUR

TABLES OF FOUR	
Advantage	**Disadvantage**
Effective for the following instructiona *strategies/activities*	

ACTIVITY C

CREATING RULES & PROCEDURES (FEAP 2)

Part 1 Directions: Create three rules, with consequences, for your class. Identify positive reinforcements you will provide for each rule.

Rule 1/Expectation: _____

_____

Positive Reinforcement: _____

Consequence for Breaking Rule: _____

_____

Rule 2/Expectation: _____

_____

Positive Reinforcement: _____

Consequence for Breaking Rule: _____

_____

Rule 3/Expectation: _____

_____

Positive Reinforcement: _____

Consequence for Breaking Rule: _____

_____

Part 2 Directions: Create three procedures related to tasks (such as getting materials and turning in assignments) that will help you to run your class efficiently.

Procedure 1: _____

Procedure 2: _____

Procedure 3: _____

Part 3 Directions: Write the rules and procedures on poster board and display them in your class. Orally present and explain the rules and procedures to your students. Model the rules and procedures and then have your students model them.

- Attach a picture of the poster board displaying your rules and procedures to this activity.
- Did your students understand the rules and procedures when you explained them? Why or why not?

_____

_____

_____

- After reflecting on your rules, consequences, positive reinforcements, and procedures, what, if any, would you change?

_____

_____

_____

_____

_____

_____

ACTIVITY D

STUDENT NEEDS & INSTRUCTIONAL DECISIONS (FEAP 2)

Teachers must address each student's cognitive, linguistic, social, emotional, and physical development.

Identify a student in your class. What instructional decisions will you need to make in order to meet this student's needs?

Student's Name: _____

1. Which area(s) of development need(s) to be addressed?

    O   Cognitive

    O   Linguistic

    O   Social

    O   Emotional

    O   Physical

2. The instructional decisions I need to make:

    _____

    _____

    _____

    _____

    _____

ACTIVITY E

LEP JOURNAL ABSTRACT (FEAP 2)

Familiarize yourself with theories, strategies, and techniques utilized in the classroom to implement effective Limited English Proficient (LEP) strategies by reading an article from a current professional education journal related to LEP strategies.

Summarize the content of the article by emphasizing the key theories, strategies, techniques, etc. Relate these ideas to your experiences.

Explain how the knowledge you gained from reading an article about LEP strategies will impact your teaching and improve student achievement.

ACTIVITY F

INTEGRATION OF TECHNOLOGY (FEAP 2)

The purpose of this activity is to identify a resource (WebQuests, PowerPoint, Virtual Fieldtrips, Assistive Technology, etc.) you can use to integrate current information and communication technologies into your lesson.

1. Identify the specific technological resource.

   _____

2. Give a brief overview of the technological resource.

   _____

   _____

   _____

Activity # 1

Subject area _____ Grade _____

Name of activity: _____

Describe the activity you have chosen or developed and discuss specifically how you will implement it in your specific subject area.

List materials needed by the student and the teacher.

Explain how this activity improves student achievement.

Explain how this activity is related to the technological resource you selected.

Activity # 2

Subject area _____ Grade _____

Name of activity: _____

Describe the activity you have chosen or developed and discuss specifically how you will implement it in your specific subject area.

List materials needed by the student and the teacher.

Explain how this activity improves student achievement.

Explain how this activity is related to the technological resource you selected.

RESOURCES

Albert, L. (1989). *Cooperative discipline: Classroom management that promotes self-esteem*. Circle Pines, MN: American Guidance Service Publishing.

Baviskar, S., Hartle, R., & Whitney, T. (2009). Essential criteria to characterize constructivist teaching: Derived from a review of the literature and applied to five constructivist teaching method articles. *International Journal of Science Education*, 31(4), 541-550.

Canter, L. & Canter, M. (2002). Assertive discipline: Positive behavior management for today's schools. Bloomington, IN: Solution Tree.

Cavanaugh, C.; Gillan, K.; Kromrey, J., Hess, M. & Blomeyer, R. (2004). *The effects of distance education on K–12 student outcomes: A meta-analysis*. Retrieved June 5, 2010, from http://www.ncrel.org/tech/distance/k12distance.pdf

Cowan, J. (2008). Strategies for planning technology-enhanced learning experiences. *The Clearing House*, 82(5), 55-9.

Cross, N. (2008). The power of expectations. *Principal Leadership*, 9(3), 24-28.

Danielson, C. (2007, 2nd edition). *Enhancing professional practice: A framework for teaching.* Alexandria, VA: Association for Supervision and Curriculum Development.

Domains: Knowledge base of the Florida Performance Measurement System. (2002). [Third Revised Edition]. Retrieved August 6, 2010, from http://www.duvalschools.org/newteachers/FPMS/FPMS%20Domain%20-%20CD%20Version.pdf

Florida Department of Children and Families. (n.d.). *Florida abuse hotline*. Retrieved May 2, 2010, from http://www.dcf.state.fl.us/abuse/definitions.shtml

Florida Department of Education. *Florida's bullying prevention project*. Retrieved May 2, 2010, from http://www.fldoe.org/safeschools/bullying.asp

Florida Department of Education. (2008, July 11). *Model policy against bullying and harassment.* Retrieved May 2, 2010 from http://www.fldoe.org/safeschools/bullying_prevention.asp

Florida Department of Education. (2010). *6A-5.065-The Educator Accomplished Practices as approved by the State Board of Education on December 17, 2010.* Retrieved December 21, 2010, from http://www.fldoe.org/profdev/FEAPSRevisions/

Index of learning theories and models. Retrieved March 18, 2010, from http://www.learning-theories.com/

Kelly, K. & Killy, M. (1989). *Mother's almanac II*. New York: Doubleday.

Kingsley, K. V. (2007). Empower diverse learners with educational technology and digital media. *Intervention in School & Clinic, 43*(1), 52-56.

Lezotte, L. (1991). *Correlates of effective schools: The first and second generation*. Okemos, MI: Effective Schools Products, Ltd..

Lezotte, L. (n.d.). *Effective schools: Past, present, and future*. Retrieved March 19, 2010, from http://www.effectiveschools.com/images/stories/brockpaper.pdf

Martin, N., Yin, Z. & Baldwin, B. (1998, April). *Classroom management training, class size and graduate study: Do these variables impact teachers' beliefs regarding classroom management style?* Paper presented at the annual conference of the American Educational Research Association.

McInerney, D. E. (2000). *Helping kids achieve their best: Understanding and using motivation in the classroom.* St. Leonards, N.S.W.: Allen & Unwin.

MacKenzie, R.J. & Stanzione, L. (2010). *Setting limits in the classroom: A complete guide to effective classroom management with a school-wide discipline plan.* NY: Three Rivers Press.

Marzano, R. J. (2007). *The Art and science of teaching*. Alexandria, VA: Association for Supervision and Curriculum Development.

National Association of State Boards of Education. (2001). *Any time, any place, any path, any pace: Taking the lead on e-learning policy*. Alexandria, VA: author.

National Center for Education Statistics. (2010). *Indicator 11: Bullying at school and cyber-bullying anywhere.* Retrieved January 2, 2011, from http://nces.ed.gov/programs/crimeindicators/crimeindicators2010/ind_11.asp

National Center for Education Statistics. (2010). *Indicator 7: Discipline problems reported by public schools.* Retrieved January 2, 2011, from http://nces.ed.gov/programs/crimeindicators/crimeindicators2010/tables/table_07_1.asp

Owens, R., Hester, J., & Teale, W. (2002). Where do you want to go today? Inquiry-based learning and technology integration: Providing a choice of subjects to study and a range of new technologies with which to study them produced positive results in two programs. *The Reading Teacher, 55*(7), 616-621.

Pennington, M. (2008, November 2). *Characteristics of high school learners*. Retrieved April 18, 2010, from http://ezinearticles.com/?Characteristics-of-High-School-Learners&id=1641532

Pennington, M. (2009, January 3). *Characteristics of middle school learners.* Retrieved April 18, 2010, from http://ezinearticles.com/?Characteristics-of-Middle-School-Learners&id=1843077

Reeve, J. & Halusic, M. (2009). How K-12 teachers can put self-determination theory principles into practice. *Theory and Research in Education, 7*(2), 145-154.

Sampson, R. (2009). Bullying in schools. *Community Oriented Policing Services, U. S. Department of Justice,* (12).

Seifert, T. L. (2004). Understanding student motivation. *Educational Research, 46*(2).

Sprick, R. (2009). Doing discipline differently. *Principal Leadership*, 9(5), 18-22.

Tauber, R. (2007). *Classroom management: Sound theory and effective practice.* Westport, CT: Praeger Publishers.

U.S. Department of Education. (n.d.). *Effects of technology on classrooms and students.* Retrieved June 1, 2010, from http://www2.ed.gov/pubs/EdReformStudies/EdTech/effectsstudents.html

Williams, R. (1999). The behavioral perspective in contemporary education. *The Teacher Educator, 35*(2), 44-60.

Watson, J. (2007, April). *A national primer on K-12 online learning.* Retrieved June 5, 2010, from http://www.inacol.org/research/docs/national_report.pdf

Watson, J.; Gemin, B.; Ryan, J.; and Wicks, M. (2009, November) *Keeping pace with K-12 online learning.* Retrieved June 5, 2010, from http://www.kpk12.com/downloads/KeepingPace09-fullreport.pdf

INSTRUCTIONAL DELIVERY AND FACILITATION

The effective educator consistently utilizes a deep and comprehensive knowledge of the subject taught to:

- Deliver engaging and challenging lessons
- Deepen and enrich students' understanding through content area literacy strategies, verbalization of thought, and application of the subject matter
- Identify gaps in students' subject matter knowledge
- Modify instruction to respond to preconceptions or misconceptions
- Relate and integrate the subject matter with other disciplines and life experiences
- Employ higher-order questioning techniques
- Apply varied instructional strategies and resources, including appropriate technology, to provide comprehensible instruction and to teach for student understanding
- Differentiate instruction based on an assessment of student learning needs and recognition of individual differences in students
- Support, encourage, and provide immediate and specific feedback to students to promote student achievement
- Utilize student feedback to monitor instructional needs and to adjust instruction

Florida Educator Accomplished Practice #3:

INSTRUCTIONAL DELIVERY AND FACILITATION

DID YOU KNOW...

Introduction:
Teachers are expected to be experts in teaching methods, child development, managing children, and, of course, in their subject areas. Society takes for granted that teachers know their "stuff" and are able to pass on knowledge to all their students successfully.

Vocabulary:

academic rule – a form of knowledge consisting of a man-made, operational statement; often found in mathematics, language arts, and science; the word "always" often appears in the rule

Bloom's Taxonomy – Bloom's classification of behavior in the cognitive domain; from simple to complex, it consists of knowledge, comprehension, application, analysis, synthesis and evaluation; updated to consist of remembering, understanding, applying, analyzing, evaluating and creating

Bloom's Taxonomy revised – Bloom's Revised Taxonomy of cognitive objectives consists of remembering, understanding, applying, analyzing, evaluating, and creating

computer-assisted instruction – instruction delivered by a computer including tutorial, simulation, drill, and practice; an example is Accelerated Reader

computer-managed instruction – the use of a computer system to manage information about learner performance and learning-resources options in order to prescribe and control individual lessons

concept – a form of knowledge that consists of a definition, attributes, examples, and non-examples

cooperative learning – an instructional strategy whereby students work in cooperative groups to achieve a common goal; conditions that promote effective cooperative learning include positive interdependence among group members, face-to-face interaction, clearly perceived individual accountability to achieve the group's goals, frequent use of interpersonal skills, and regular group processing to improve the group's functioning

core curriculum – subject or discipline components of the curriculum considered as being absolutely necessary, including English/language arts, mathematics, science, and history/social studies

critical thinking – higher-level thinking used to analyze, synthesize, and evaluate

cultural forces – four teaching strategies used to help students acquire thinking skills: (1) providing models of the culture, (2) explaining important cultural knowledge, (3) providing interaction among students and other members of the cultural community, and (4) providing feedback on students' use of thinking skills

cultural pluralism – a view of diversity that embraces cultural differences

culture – a way of life in which people share a common language and similar values, religion, ideals, habits of thinking, artistic expressions, and patterns of social and interpersonal relations

curriculum tracking – the practice of students' voluntary or involuntary placement in different programs or courses according to their abilities and prior academic performance

dimensions of good thinking – six aspects that characterize skill in thinking critically; include a language of thinking, thinking dispositions, mental management, a strategic spirit, higher-order knowledge, and transfer

document camera – a type of overhead projector that can project solid paper or transparencies

educational psychology – the scientific study of the teaching-learning process

encoding – a process of relating new information to prior knowledge so that it can be later retrieved and used

expository learning – the traditional classroom instructional approach that proceeds as follows: presentation of information to the learners, reference to particular examples, and application of the information to the learners' experiences

hidden curriculum – the accepted or implied values and attitudes and the unwritten rules of behavior students must learn to participate and to be successful in school

high-yield strategies – presented by Robert Marzano; instructional strategies that usually improve student achievement

interdisciplinary teaching – two or more subject areas are integrated to examine a central theme, issue, topic, experience, or problem

interdisciplinary team – an organizational pattern of two or more teachers representing different subject areas; the team shares the same students, schedule, areas of the school, and the opportunity for teaching more than one subject

knowledge base of teaching – the source from which a theory of teaching can be reflectively constructed; that which is known from educational psychology and classroom practice

law – a form of knowledge derived from a scientific generalization that is based on physical behavior or empirical observations

law-like principle – a form of knowledge based on a procedural principle that is applicable only in a particular domain; usually uses linking words such as "if" and "then"

learning – change in thought or behavior that modifies a person's capabilities

lesson initiation – statement by the teacher at the beginning of the lesson that orients students to the topic and/or academic activity

management transition – organized manner in which a teacher shifts from one activity to another; teacher frequently uses words such as "now" and "next"

metaphor – a way to represent and talk about experiences in terms of other, more familiar, or more commonly shared events that seem comparable

multilevel instruction – when several levels of teaching and learning are going on simultaneously in the same classroom, when students are working on different objectives, or when different students are doing various tasks leading to the same objective; also called multitasking

orient – comments made by the teacher prior to the lesson or activity to gather the attention of the students; an example is "Everyone, look at the picture on page 10 of your book."

pragmatics – the contexts in which language is used and the way in which language can be used to create contexts

presentation software – a computer software package used to display information, normally in the form of a slide show; an example would be PowerPoint

reflective abstraction – process by which logical-mathematical knowledge is generated; thinking by means of purely mental operations

reflective construction – thinking critically about the principles and concepts of educational psychology and classroom practice in order to develop a theory of teaching

reframing – rethinking an event or problem in terms of metaphors in order to gain a new perspective

Response to Intervention (RTI) – the practice of modifying instruction and implementing interventions based on individual needs of students; ultimate goal is student success

schemata – theoretical knowledge structures that contain information, facts, principles, and the relationships among them

search engine – a web site used to search for information on the World Wide Web; the search results are usually presented in a list; examples are Google and Bing

short-term memory – phase of processing information in which a limited amount of information is stored for a limited time

teaching – planned arrangement of experiences to help a learner achieve a desirable change in behavior or an understanding; also called instruction

teaching strategy – a method used by the teacher to facilitate learning; some strategies are traditional (lectures, class discussions), while others are more creative (WebQuests)

teaching style – the way a teacher teaches, including any distinctive mannerisms and personal choices of teaching behaviors and strategies

teaching-learning process – the process of taking action to produce change in thought or behavior and subsequent modification of capabilities

the Net – slang term for the Internet

theory of teaching – description, explanations, and prediction of actions taken with the intent to facilitate learning

value knowledge – a form of knowledge that leads students to examine the work of an event, idea, or behavior; the teacher guides students in identifying judgmental criteria, listing pros and cons, researching facts, and reaching a consensus

Webb's Depth of Knowledge levels – created by Norman Webb, consists of four levels of mental processing teachers should use for instruction—recall (level 1), skill/concept (level 2), strategic thinking (level 3), and extended thinking (level four)

WebQuest – an inquiry-based on-line group learning activity where students gather information from a variety of Internet sources and then apply the new knowledge to explain a concept

wiki – a website that allows the easy creation and editing of any number of interlinked web pages via a web browser; used to enhance group learning and for personal note taking

word processor software – a computer application used for the production (including composition, editing, formatting, and possibly printing) of any sort of printable material; an example is WORD

WHY WE KNOW...

Research

Teachers must have content knowledge of the discipline(s) they teach. To be successful in the classroom, though, they must also be able to present the knowledge in ways that make it comprehensible to students. This includes understanding which topics are easy or difficult for students to learn, which teaching strategies are more likely to be successful, and the prior knowledge their students are bringing to the classroom (Shulman, 1986).

Teachers must also ensure their students can learn the content by teaching them the academic vocabulary associated with the lesson. According to Marzano (2005), students find it easier to understand information they read and hear in class if their teachers introduced them to the vocabulary words prior to or during the lesson.

FORMS OF KNOWLEDGE

To present content effectively, the teacher needs to identify the form(s) of knowledge that will be used during the lesson presentation.

Concepts: A concept is a group or category to which objects, ideas, or events belong. As a form of knowledge, it must be presented to students with a definition, attributes, examples, and non-examples.

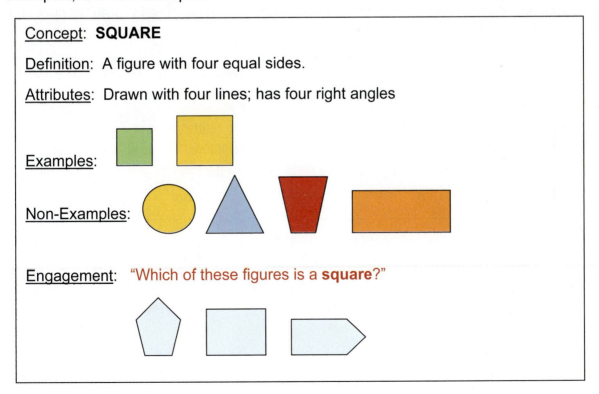

Concept: **SQUARE**

Definition: A figure with four equal sides.

Attributes: Drawn with four lines; has four right angles

Examples:

Non-Examples:

Engagement: "Which of these figures is a **square**?"

Law: A law is a scientific generalization based on physical behavior or empirical observations. When teaching a law, state the formal law, its causes/effects, and give students an opportunity to apply the law.

Law: The sun rises in the east and sets in the west.

Engagement: "You live in Miami, your aunt lives in Dallas, and your grandmother lives in Los Angeles. All of you set your alarm clock for 7:30 a.m. Who will be the first person to wake up? Explain your answer."

Newton's first Law: "Every object persists in its state of rest or uniform motion in a straight line unless it is compelled to change that state by forces impressed on it."

Engagement: Have students move objects on their desks and use their hands to stop the movement.

Law-like Principle: A law-like principle is a procedural principle that is applicable only in a particular domain and usually uses linking words such as "if" and "then" to show the cause and effect relationship.

Law-like Principle: "If the President doesn't have the support of Congress (then), he can't get his favorite legislation passed."

Engagement: "The majority of Representatives and Senators are fiscal conservatives. The President wants to increase the federal budget, which will result in a 10% increase of the nation's debt. Evaluate the President's chances of getting what he wants."

Academic Rule: An academic rule is a statement that is man-made, operational, and most often found in mathematics, language arts, and science. The word "always" often appears in the rule.   Remember to use the word "when" before you state the rule, then issue the rule command. Provide students with an opportunity to apply the rule through class activities.

Academic Rule: When writing a sentence, always capitalize the first letter of the sentence.

Engagement: "Using this rule, correct the following sentences."

1. will you be able to play?
2. please read the book.
3. place your pencil on the desk.

Value Knowledge: Value knowledge refers to the presentation of content that leads students to examine the work of an event, idea, or behavior. The teacher's role is to guide the students in identifying judgmental criteria, listing pros and cons, researching the facts, and reaching a consensus.

Value Knowledge: Is capital punishment an effective means of deterring crime in our society?

Engagement: "What does 'effective' mean?" *(Students participate to form a definition.)*

Students research the pros and cons of capital punishment, sharing their research with the rest of the class.

Based upon the research and class discussion, students determine whether capital punishment is an effective *means of deterring crime.*

INTERDISCIPLINARY TEACHING

Interdisciplinary teaching involves integrating two or more subject areas while examining a central theme, issue, topic, experience, or problem. The content of the subjects and the skills are intertwined.

Example: The language arts teacher assigns the book *The Watsons Go to Birmingham: 1963* for her students to read (language arts, reading comprehension, vocabulary). The students draw a map representing the main character's trip from Flint, Michigan, to Birmingham, Alabama, and the distance of the trip (geography, reading a map, determining distance). Students compare the cost of the trip in 1963 when gas cost 25 cents to the cost of gas today (math skills). The Civil Rights movement is discussed (social studies).

MODIFYING INSTRUCTION TO ADDRESS PRECONCEPTIONS AND MISCONCEPTIONS

Sometimes students fail to grasp new concepts and information because of their preconceptions and misconceptions about how the world works (Donovan & Bransford, 2005). Teachers must identify these gaps in knowledge and modify instruction to help their students understand new material.

Example of a Preconception:

The elementary teacher tells the students to refer to the "model" to answer questions about the solar system. Students in the class believe the word "model" refers to a person wearing designer clothing.

Modification of Instruction:

The teacher picks up the model of the solar system and explains that a model can be a representation of an idea or object.

Example of a Misconception:

The middle school teacher has just completed a unit on plants. The teacher gives each student a graphic organizer with instructions to compare animals to plants. While circulating the room, the teacher notices that several students wrote, "plants are not alive."

Modification of Instruction:

The teacher explains why plants are "alive".

INSTRUCTIONAL STRATEGIES

An instructional strategy is a method used by the teacher to facilitate learning. Some strategies are traditional (lectures, class discussions), while others are more creative (WebQuests).

Research has shown that learning is enhanced when teachers use instructional strategies that meet the needs and interests of their students. Therefore, all instructional strategies must be linked to the curriculum and the desired student outcomes. A balance should exist between active and passive instructional strategies.

Skillful teachers orient students to gain their attention prior to the lesson or activity. Examples of orienting students include:

- "Turn to page 20 of your textbook and look at question number one."
- "Class, look at the upper left hand corner of your monitor."
- "Everyone, look at the second paragraph on your handout".

CATEGORIES OF INSTRUCTIONAL STRATEGIES

In *Models of Teaching* (Joyce & Weil, 1986), four major categories of teaching strategies were identified. The categories are:
- <u>Social</u>—helping students study and learn together (cooperative learning, peer teaching, group investigation)
- <u>Personal</u>—emphasizing the development of personal growth and creativity (nondirective teaching, problem-based instruction)
- <u>Information Processing</u>—presenting information so that students can learn and retain information more effectively (advance organizers, mnemonics)
- <u>Behavioral Systems</u>—helping students acquire basic information and skills (simulations, e-learning)

When selecting an instructional strategy, the teacher needs to consider time, physical space, equipment/supplies, and class size.

CONTENT AREA LITERACY STRATEGIES

Literacy instruction does not end at the elementary level. Secondary teachers need to help their students acquire vocabulary, comprehension, writing, and study skills specific to their content area and grade level. Therefore, teachers need to use instructional strategies that will help their students learn the content relevant to the subject area taught. The *Content Area Literacy Guide* (Public Consulting Group's Center for Resource Management, 2007) suggests the following to help core knowledge teachers address concerns with reading and writing in their subject areas.

SUBJECT AREA	ROADBLOCKS TO LEARNING	INSTRUCTIONAL STRATEGIES TO SUPPORT LITERACY
Science	• technical vocabulary • symbols and formulas • expository writing style	• vocabulary development activities • use of leveled texts • use of text supplements • lab experiments • graphic organizers
Social Studies	• graphs, maps, various presentations of data • the need to recognize bias and distinguish fact from opinion	• questioning strategies • move from cause and effect relationships to persuasive and argumentative essays • report writing of an event • defending an idea or belief • graphic organizers
Mathematics	• technical vocabulary • symbols, equations, graphic representations • the need to be an analytical reader	• direct instruction • discuss and investigate solutions • decode words and numeric and nonnumeric symbols • translate words into problems and problems into words
Language Arts	• literary devices • teacher-assigned reading lists	• literature circles • collaborative learning groups • graphic organizers

ADVANTAGES AND DISADVANTAGES OF
MOST COMMON INSTRUCTIONAL METHODS

Effective teachers use different strategies for presenting subject content. Below are the most common strategies, along with the advantages and disadvantages of each (McCarthy, 1992).

Lecture

Preparation: Need introduction and summary
Need appropriate time and content
Should include examples and anecdotes

Advantages	Disadvantages
Useful for large groups	Very little engagement by the learner
Easy to prepare	Difficult to measure learning
Good for presenting background information when it is not available or accessible to the students	One-way communication (teacher does all the talking)

Lecture with Discussion

Preparation: Requires questions be prepared prior to discussion

Advantages	Disadvantages
Students are involved after the lecture	Time limits may reduce discussion period
Students can ask clarifying questions	Quality of discussion is limited to the quality of the questions

Class Discussion

Preparation: Requires careful planning by teacher to guide discussion
Requires question outline

Advantages	Disadvantages
Ideas and experiences are shared by students	Not practical for groups larger than 20
All students can participate	Class may get side tracked

Small Group Discussion

Preparation: Requires specific tasks and questions to be prepared in advance

Advantages	Disadvantages
All students participate	Groups may get off topic
Some students feel more comfortable in small groups	Teacher has to move from group to group to monitor progress
Groups can reach consensus	

Worksheets

Preparation: Requires advanced preparation

Advantages	Disadvantages
Allows students to work independently or in groups	Can be used for only a short period of time
Can be created to target the exact skill or concept being taught	Costly to purchase or to make class copies
Can be saved for future use	

Videotapes/DVDs

Preparation: Requires equipment set up in advance
Students need to understand what they should be looking for when they watch the video

Advantages	Disadvantages
Entertaining and usually keeps students' attention	Equipment may fail
Can pause the tape to get student involvement	Effective only if followed by questions related to the video

ADVANTAGES AND DISADVANTAGES OF
MORE CREATIVE INSTRUCTIONAL STRATEGIES

Brainstorming

Preparation: Teacher selects topic

Advantages	Disadvantages
Encourages critical thinking by students	Needs to have a time limit
One idea can generate other ideas	Must be facilitated or criticism of student input may occur
Draws on knowledge and experiences of students	Some students may try to take over the discussion

Case Studies

Preparation: Case studies must be clearly defined and prepared in advance

Advantages	Disadvantages
Encourages critical thinking and problem-solving skills	Insufficient information can lead to poor results
Students can apply new knowledge and skills	Not appropriate for elementary level
Provides opportunity for students to assume the roles of others	

Graphic Organizers

Preparation: Requires advanced preparation

Advantages	Disadvantages
Provides opportunity for critical thinking	Costly to purchase or to make copies
Encourages problem solving	
Supports material presented by the teacher	

Internet

Preparation: Requires computer availability and access to the Internet

Advantages	Disadvantages
Provides opportunity for students to do research	Teachers have to be aware of web sites accessed by students
Can be used to support content presented by teacher	Depending upon size of class, students may have to share computers
Provides opportunity for students to practice technology skills	

Role Playing

Preparation: Teacher must define roles and problem/situation clearly
Instructions must be very clear

Advantages	Disadvantages
Provides opportunity for students to assume roles of others	Some students may be too self-conscious
Encourages problem solving	Only appropriate for small groups
Provides opportunity for students to practice skills	Some students may feel threatened

WebQuest

Preparation: Teacher must provide specific guidelines for the WebQuest

Advantages	Disadvantages
Provides opportunity for students to use technology	Students may just surf the net
Helps students to have "real world" experiences	Depending upon size of class, students may have to share computers
Provides opportunity for students to practice problem-solving skills	Time-consuming activity

WHAT YOU NEED TO KNOW...

In *Classroom Instruction That Works: Research Based Strategies for Increasing Student Achievement* (2001), Marzano, et. al., identify nine "high yield" instructional strategies that usually improve student achievement. They emphasize, however, that teachers should always rely on their knowledge of their own students before selecting specific instructional strategies.

HIGH YIELD INSTRUCTIONAL STRATEGIES

The "High-Yield" strategies are listed below:

Identifying Similarities and Differences
- Break a concept into similar and dissimilar characteristics
- Use graphic organizers to help students understand

Summarizing and Note Taking
- Use a consistent format for notes
- Ask students to question what is unclear
- *(Avoid the use of verbatim note taking because students do not have time to process the information)*

Reinforce Effort and Provide Recognition
- Share stories about people who succeeded
- Give awards for individual accomplishments
- Have students keep a log of their efforts and achievements

Homework and Practice
- Assign amount of homework based on grade level
- Allow only minimal parental involvement on homework
- Give feedback on all homework
- Maximize effectiveness of feedback by varying the way it is delivered

Nonlinguistic Representations
- Incorporate works and images to represent relationships
- Use models and physical movement to represent information

Setting Objectives and Providing Feedback
- Use contracts to identify specific goals students must attain to earn a grade
- Make sure feedback is corrective in nature
- Encourage students to lead feedback sessions

Generating and Testing Hypotheses
- Have students explain their hypotheses and conclusions
- Ask students to predict
- Ask students to build something using limited resources (why it did or did not work?)

Cues, Questions and Advance Organizers
- Help students use what they know to enhance further learning
- Ask questions that are highly analytical and focus on what is important

Cooperative Learning Groups
- Set up learning groups in which students can cooperate with one another

What is a Cooperative Learning Group?

Cooperative Learning is a collaborative learning model that requires students to work and talk together about academic material, while learning effective, positive interpersonal skills.

- 2 – 5 students are working together toward a common goal
- Each member of the group assumes a role or has a task
- Members are of mixed backgrounds and capabilities
- Cooperative Learning is NOT breaking the class into small groups for an activity

Five Basic Elements of Cooperative Learning:
- Positive interdependence
- Face-to-face interaction
- Individual accountability
- Interpersonal and small group skills
- Group processing

Cooperative Learning Groups should be used in lessons involving:
- problem solving,
- investigations,
- experiments, and
- projects.

What are the roles of the teacher when using Cooperative Learning Groups?

- Identify the objective of the activity.
- Identify interpersonal and small group skills that will be assessed.
- Determine the number of students in each cooperative group and the roles students will have.
- Teach skills before giving out the assignment. The skills are:
    Social Skills—active listening, sharing of materials, taking turns, giving support;
    Explaining Skills—students can describe a problem, ask others for help in understanding content; and
    Leadership Skills—initiative, planning, and enthusiasm (assign a leader).

- Plan the room arrangement to facilitate face-to-face interaction (group tables or desks).
- Establish procedures for the activity.
- Monitor progress and direction of the groups (make sure everyone is participating).
- Manage talking (students will get louder so attention signals will be needed) and on-task behavior.
- Assess the quality of the group work and hold individuals accountable for the task. Consider giving group and individual grades.
- Conduct a brief group reflection during the last 3-5 minutes of the activity to discuss how students effectively worked together.

What can be the group members' roles?

- *Group Facilitator*—student keeps members of group on task
- *Materials Manager*—student obtains, maintains, and returns group's materials
- *Recorder*—student keeps record of all of group's activities
- *Reporter*—student tells teacher (or class) of group's accomplishments
- *Thinking Monitor*—student explains how group arrived at answer

According to research, Cooperative Learning Groups:
- promote student learning and achievement,
- increase student retention of material,
- encourage more active (versus passive) participation,
- increase the use of higher level reasoning skills,
- promote higher self-esteem,
- improve student communication, and
- result in fewer off-task behaviors.

COLLABORATIVE LEARNING

Research has indicated that students working in small groups, such as collaborative learning, are more likely to learn and retain the information presented by the teacher (Davis, 1993).

Before teachers use collaborative learning groups, they need to:
- carefully identify the assignment the students will be asked to accomplish (solve a problem, complete a task, or create a product),
- teach students the skills they will need to succeed in groups (active listening, helping others, and giving or receiving constructive criticism),
- decide how the group will operate, and
- determine how students will be graded.

Student benefits from collaborative learning include:
- the development of higher level thinking skills,
- the development of oral communication skills,
- a more positive attitude toward the subject matter,
- the development of social interaction skills, and
- reduction of classroom anxiety.

USING CRITICAL THINKING STRATEGIES TO IMPROVE
THE QUALITY OF INSTRUCTION

Is education just learning the facts, or is it being able to apply the facts in new situations? Lectures and memorization were the most common methods of teaching used in classrooms for decades. Noticing that students were lagging in problem-solving and thinking skills, critics called for teachers to engage their students by delivering challenging lessons.

BLOOM'S TAXONOMY

In 1956, Benjamin Bloom led a group of educational psychologists who found that over 95% of the test questions students encountered required them to think only at the lowest possible level—the recall of information.

Bloom identified six levels of cognitive thinking that revolve around knowledge, comprehension, and critical thinking. These levels are Knowledge, Comprehension, Application, Analysis, Synthesis, and Evaluation.

- **Knowledge**—identifying previously-learned information (recall)

- **Comprehension**—organizing and selecting facts and ideas

- **Application**—solving problems to new situations by using previously acquired knowledge, facts, and/or principles

- **Analysis**—examining or breaking information into parts to find evidence to support generalizations

- **Synthesis**—combining information in a different way to create a new pattern or an alternative solution

- **Evaluation**—developing opinions, judgments, or decisions based on a set of criteria

In 2001, Lorin Anderson and a group of cognitive psychologists, curriculum theorists, and instructional researchers revised Bloom's taxonomy to reflect relevance to the 21st century (Anderson, 2001). The new levels are described below.

- **Remember**—recalling, recognizing, and retrieving knowledge from long-term memory

- **Understand**—developing meaning from oral, written, and graphic information through classifying, exemplifying, inferring, interpreting, summarizing, comparing, and explaining

- **Apply**—using a procedure through executing or implementing

- **Analyze**—breaking information into parts, determining how the parts relate to one another and to an overall structure or purpose by differentiating, organizing, and attributing

- **Evaluate**—making judgments based on criteria and standards by checking and critiquing

- **Create**—putting elements together to form a functional whole; reorganizing elements into a new pattern or structure by generating, planning, or producing

WEBB'S DEPTH OF KNOWLEDGE

Norman Webb's Depth of Knowledge (DOK) levels explore the complexity of mental processing that must occur to answer a question. Unlike Bloom's, Taxonomy what follows the verb in the Depth of Knowledge levels is more important than the verb itself (Webb, 2005). The DOK levels are:

- **Level 1—Recall/Reproduction** (of a fact, information, concept, or procedure)

- **Level 2–Skill/Concept** (using information or conceptual knowledge, solving problems in two or more steps, organizing and displaying data)

- **Level 3—Strategic Thinking** (requiring reasoning, developing a plan or a sequence of steps involving some complexity, requiring decision making and justification, involving abstract and complex thinking with more than one possible answer)

- **Level 4—Extended Thinking** (requiring an investigation or research using multiple sources, using time to think and process multiple conditions of the problem, requiring complex reasoning)

SAMPLE ACTIVITIES FOR WEBB'S DEPTH OF KNOWLEDGE

DEPTH OF KNOWLEDGE	EXAMPLE
Level 1	Measure the length of your desk.
Level 2	Take the water temperature of the school's pond every day for a month. Construct a graph to represent your data.
Level 3	What conclusions can you draw from the data you were provided regarding global warming? Cite evidence to support your conclusion.
Level 4	Describe and illustrate common art themes found in various cultures.

STRATEGIES PROMOTING CRITICAL & CREATIVE THINKING SKILLS

Teachers need to provide activities that promote critical and creative thinking skills. This is especially important since state assessments contain higher order questions. To encourage students to use their imagination and become engaged in the learning process, teachers can use the following strategies.

A-B-C Summarize—assigning each student a different letter of the alphabet, then students select a word starting with that letter that is related to the topic being discussed

Analyzing—examining information (breaking up the whole into its parts) to find important elements or criteria

Carousel—Collaborative problem-solving using teams of three students

Comparing and Contrasting—examining objects or ideas in order to identify attributes that make them similar and/or different

Deductive Reasoning—drawing a conclusion from facts

Decision Making—selecting one of several options after consideration of facts or ideas, possible alternatives, probable consequences, and personal values

Drawing Conclusions—summarizing ideas, materials, and thoughts and arriving at decisions based on reasoning and inferences

Evaluating—making a judgment based on a set of criteria

Grab Bag—Near the end of a lesson, students draw an object from a bag. Student must explain how the object is related to what they learned.

Inductive Reasoning—combining one or more assumptions or hypotheses with available information to come to a general conclusion

Identifying Attributes—recognizing and selecting characteristics, properties, or qualities shared by all members of the same set

Identifying Cause and Effect—identifying why an event occurred and the numerous consequences of the event

Interpreting—explaining, defining, and appraising the meaning of a situation

Making Inferences—drawing conclusions based on available, but incomplete, information or facts

Observing—using senses to gather information

Pair Problem Solving—dividing the class into pairs; one member of the pair, the "thinker," thinks aloud as he/she tries to solve a problem. The other member of the pair, the "listener," analyzes and provides feedback on the "thinker's" approach for solving the problem.

Patterning—arranging objects, conditions, events, or ideas according to a repeated scheme

Sequencing—arranging events, items, or objects in some order (ascending or descending) according to some relevant quality

GRAPHIC ORGANIZERS

A graphic organizer is a visual representation of knowledge, concepts, or ideas. They are used to promote understanding and assist students in organizing their thoughts. The following are examples:

- **KWL** – Before a topic is presented, students are asked to identify what they **K**now about the topic and what they **W**ant to know about the topic. After the lesson, the students are asked to identify what they **L**earned.

What I KNOW	What I WANT to Know	What I LEARNED
1.	1.	1.
2.	2.	2.
3.	3.	3.
4.	4.	4.
5.	5.	5.
6.	6.	6.

- **Venn Diagram** – This diagram is used to compare and contrast. Similarities are listed in the overlapping areas and differences are listed in the outer areas.

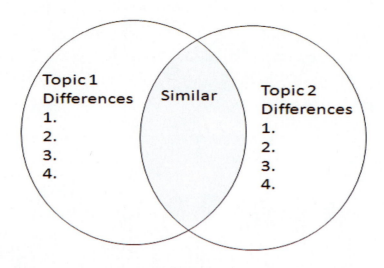

- **Thematic Web** – The main idea goes in the middle and connecting ideas or details go in connecting boxes.

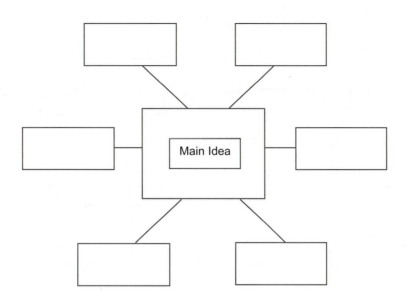

- **Concept Map** – Relationships are represented between ideas, images, or words. Concepts are usually enclosed in circles or boxes; while relationships between the concepts are indicated by a connecting line.

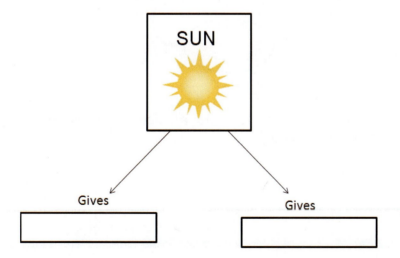

- **Cause and Effect** – The cause (an event that makes something happen) and the effects (results) of the cause are identified.

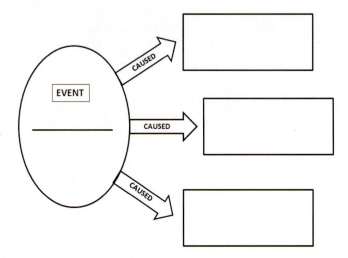

- **Cycle Diagram** – This diagram demonstrates how items are related to one another in a repeating cycle, with no absolute beginning or end.

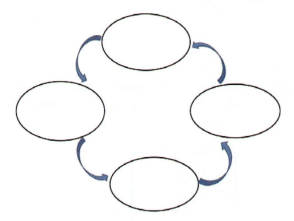

- **Timeline** – This visual is used to show a "picture" of events as they occurred during a certain period of time.

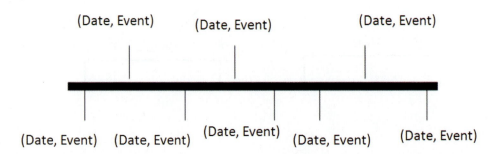

- **T-Chart** – The chart is used to compare and contrast events, people, ideas, etc., by placing individual characteristics in either the left or right section.

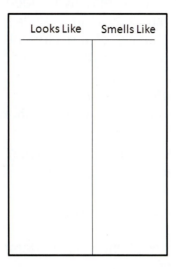

- **Story Chart** – This chart is used to help students organize the characters, setting, problem, events, and solution to a story.

STORY: _____	
Characters:	Setting When Where
Problem:	
Event 1:	
Event 2:	
Event 3:	
Solution	

FEEDBACK AND LEARNING

Teachers who provide students with effective feedback are providing them with information they can use to be successful in their learning environment. The most useful feedback focuses on the quality of the student's work and the strategies the student used to complete the work. When providing feedback, teachers should consider the following.

- Feedback is most helpful when given frequently.
- The type of feedback used (verbal or written) often depends upon the type of the assignment.
- If students are working in a group, consider giving individual and group feedback.
- Feedback needs to help students reach their goals.
- Feedback needs to be descriptive and specific.
- Feedback should not be judgmental (Brookhart, 2007).

When teachers review student work to check for understanding, they are also receiving feedback on the effectiveness of their instruction. Feedback answers the following questions:

- "Did the students master the material I taught?"
- "Do I need to re-teach any material?"
- "Which students did not master the material?"

Based on the answers to these questions, the teacher makes the decision to:

- move on to the next lesson,
- adjust instruction to re-teach material that was not learned, and/or
- provide additional assistance to students who failed to master the material.

LET IT SHOW!

Below is a list of different methods you can use to demonstrate your accomplishment of **FEAP #3: INSTRUCTIONAL DELIVERY AND FACILITATION**.

(a) Deliver engaging and challenging lessons
- ▶ <u>Research critical and creative thinking activities</u> on the Internet and incorporate them in your lessons
- ▶ <u>Create a Brain Teaser/Problem of the Day</u>: Create a brainteaser or problem based on the instructional content of your lesson plan.
- ▶ <u>Create a Lesson</u>: Create a lesson plan that uses two of Marzano's "High Yield Strategies".

(b) Deepen and enrich students' understanding through content area literacy strategies, verbalization of thought, and application of the subject matter
- ▶ <u>Use Graphic Organizers</u>: Use graphic organizers to help students understand the material presented in your lesson.
- ▶ <u>Develop a Cooperative Learning Vocabulary Activity</u>: Have students work in teams to create pictures that depict content vocabulary. Ask students to explain how the images relate to the words.

(c) Identify gaps in students' subject matter knowledge
- ▶ <u>Create a pretest/posttest</u>: Assess students prior to the lesson presentation, use the data to identify gaps in knowledge, then plan accordingly. Assess students after the lesson or unit to identify those who have meet expectations or need remediation.
- ▶ <u>Ask Questions During Your Lesson</u>: Write questions in your lesson plan that you can ask to assess whether students have learned the subject matter.

(d) Modify instruction to respond to preconceptions or misconceptions
- ▶ <u>Use a KWL Chart</u>: Before presenting a lesson, give each student a KWL graphic organizer. Tell the students to complete the "K" column (what the students *Know)* and the "W" column (What the students *"Want to Know")*. After the lesson, tell the students to complete the "L" column (What the students *Learned)*. Review the students' charts and modify instruction as needed.

(e) Relate and integrate the subject matter with other disciplines and life experiences
- ▶ <u>Create a thematic web</u> to show the relationship between subject areas and a specific concept or topic.
- ▶ <u>Create a Lesson Plan</u>: Create a lesson in which you utilize skills students have learned in another subject area.

(f) Employ higher-order questioning techniques
- ▶ <u>Plan a lesson</u> with a balance of lower and higher order questions. Write the questions in your lesson plan, so you are sure to ask them.
- ▶ <u>Create a Test</u>: Write a test with at least 50% of the questions requiring the students to apply, analyze, evaluate, and/or create.
- ▶ <u>Formulate questions</u>: Write higher order questions to ask your students during a lesson to check for understanding.
- ▶ <u>Begin a lesson</u> with an inquiry question related to your topic.
- ▶ <u>Give students the lesson topic</u> and have them create higher order questions for their peers to answer.

(g) Apply varied instructional strategies and resources, including appropriate technology, to provide comprehensive instruction, and to teach for student understanding
- ▶ <u>Identify the resources</u> available in the district, community, and school. Select those that are appropriate for your lessons and activities.
- ▶ <u>Research websites</u> and develop a resource file to use for planning units of study.
- ▶ <u>Create a WebQuest</u>: Create a WebQuest activity for your students.

(h) Differentiate instruction based on an assessment of student learning needs and recognition of individual differences in students
- ▶ <u>Teach a Lesson:</u> Teach a lesson in which you have activities that address the differing learning styles or needs of your students.
- ▶ <u>Administer a learning style inventory to your students</u> and use the results to plan assessment options.

(i) Support, encourage, and provide immediate and specific feedback to students to promote student achievement
- ▶ <u>Provide Feedback to Students</u>: During a lesson, provide verbal, academic specific feedback to a minimum of three students.
- ▶ <u>Paraphrase or repeat students responses</u> to validate their thinking and active participation in the learning process.

(j) Utilize student feedback to monitor instructional needs and to adjust instruction
- ▶ <u>Student Feedback Form</u>: At the end of the lesson, break the class into small groups. Ask each group to write down any concepts that members of the group did not understand during the lesson. Ask each group to turn in their list to you before leaving class.

ACTIVITY OVERVIEW FOR DEMONSTRATING PROFICIENCY IN
<u>FEAP #3: INSTRUCTIONAL DELIVERY AND FACILITATION</u>

(a) Deliver engaging and challenging lessons

    Activity D: WEBB'S DEPTH OF KNOWLEDGE
    Activity I: LEARNING WORDS WITH PICTURES

(b) Deepen and enrich students' understanding through content area literacy strategies, verbalization of thought, and application of the subject matter

    Activity A: CONCEPT DEVELOPMENT
    Activity I: LEARNING WORDS WITH PICTURES

(c) Identify gaps in students' subject matter knowledge

    Activity G: IDENTIFYING GAPS IN SUBJECT MATTER KNOWLEDGE

(d) Modify instruction to respond to preconceptions or misconceptions

    Activity G: IDENTIFYING GAPS IN SUBJECT MATTER KNOWLEDGE

(e) Relate and integrate the subject matter with other disciplines and life experiences

    Activity B: INTERDISCIPLINARY TEACHING ACTIVITIES

(f) Employ higher-order questioning techniques

    Activity C: BLOOM'S TAXONOMY

(g) Apply varied instructional strategies and resources, including appropriate technology, to provide comprehensive instruction, and to teach for student understanding

    Activity E: INTERNET RESOURCES
    Activity G: IDENTIFYING GAPS IN SUBJECT MATTER KNOWLEDGE

(h) Differentiate instruction based on an assessment of student learning needs and recognition of individual differences in students

Activity F: USING DIFFERENTIATED INSTRUCTION

(i) Support, encourage, and provide immediate and specific feedback to students to promote student achievement

Activity H: PROVIDING STUDENT FEEDBACK

(j) Utilize student feedback to monitor instructional needs and to adjust instruction

Activity H: PROVIDING STUDENT FEEDBACK

ACTIVITY A

CONCEPT DEVELOPMENT (FEAP 3)

A concept is a group or category to which objects, ideas or events belong.

Example: **Concept – AMPHIBIAN**

Definition – a cold-blooded vertebrate

Attributes of the definition – spends some time on land but must breed and develop into an adult in water

Examples – Frog, salamander, toad

Non-examples – turtle, alligator, fish

****

Now you do the same for the concept of **REPTILE**

Definition _____

_____

Attributes _____

Examples _____

Non-Examples _____

****

Develop your own concept _____

Definition _____

_____

Attributes _____

Examples _____

Non-Examples _____

ACTIVITY B

INTERDISCIPLINARY TEACHING ACTIVITIES (FEAP 3)

In this activity, you will create a lesson by integrating skills/knowledge from two or more subject areas.

My topic: _____

#1 Interdisciplinary Subject Area: _____

Subject Area Skill: _____

Activity in which students will use skill: _____

_____

_____

#2 Interdisciplinary Subject Area: _____

Subject Area Skill: _____

Activity in which students will use skill: _____

_____

_____

ACTIVITY C

BLOOM'S TAXONOMY (FEAP 3)

Using the "Three Little Pigs" story, create one question at each level of Bloom's Taxonomy. A table of terms at each level is provided on the following page to assist you.

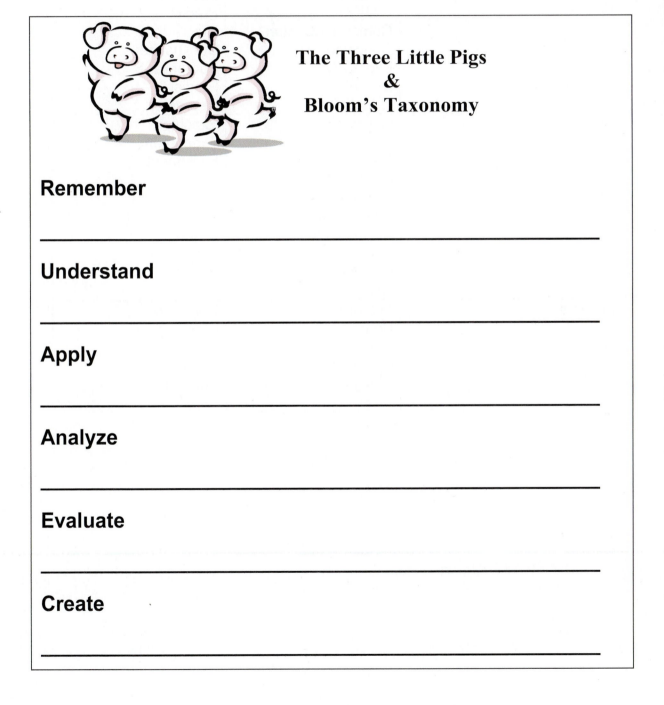

**The Three Little Pigs
&
Bloom's Taxonomy**

Remember

_____

Understand

_____

Apply

_____

Analyze

_____

Evaluate

_____

Create

_____

<u>NEW</u> BLOOM'S TAXONOMY OF THE COGNITIVE DOMAIN

LEVEL	TERMS	
Remember	Describe	Recall
	Identify	Recognize
	List	Retrieve
Understand	Categorize	Infer
	Classify	Interpret
	Clarify	Predict
	Compare / Contrast	Illustrate
	Conclude	Summarize
	Exemplify	Paraphrase
	Execute	Predict
	Generalize	Represent
Apply	Calculate	Execute
	Carry out	Experiment
	Classify	Implement
	Construct	Use
Analyze	Attribute	Explain
	Differentiate	Order
	Discriminate	Organize
Evaluate	Assess	Judge
	Conclude	Rank
	Critique	Test
Create	Actualize	Generate
	Combine	Hypothesize
	Compose	Plan
	Construct	Produce
	Design	Reorganize

ACTIVITY D

WEBB'S DEPTH OF KNOWLEDGE (FEAP 3)

Utilizing Webb's Depth of Knowledge, create activities for your students at the following levels:

- **Level 1–Recall/Reproduction** (of a fact, information, concept, or procedure)

  _____

  _____

  _____

- **Level 2–Skill/Concept** (using information or conceptual knowledge, solving problems in two or more steps, organizing and displaying data)

  _____

  _____

  _____

- **Level 3–Strategic Thinking** (requiring reasoning, developing a plan or a sequence of steps involving some complexity, requiring decision making and justification, involving abstract and complex thinking with more than one possible answer)

  _____

  _____

  _____

- **Level 4–Extended Thinking** (requiring an investigation or research using multiple sources, using time to think and process multiple conditions of the problem, requiring complex reasoning)

  _____

  _____

  _____

ACTIVITY E

INTERNET RESOURCES (FEAP 3)

The purpose of this activity is to identify web sites that will assist you in planning instruction and preparing classroom activities.

<u>Websites for Creating Lesson Plans</u>:

<u>Websites for Graphic Organizers</u>:

<u>Websites for Subject Matter Knowledge</u>:

<u>Websites for Graphics</u>:

<u>Websites for Primary Sources</u>:

<u>Websites for Activity Ideas</u>:

ACTIVITY F

USING DIFFERENTIATED INSTRUCTION (FEAP 3)

The purpose of this activity is to identify strategies you can implement to differentiate instruction and meet the needs of your students.

Part 1: Identify a topic you plan to teach: _____

_____

Part 2: Identify the strategies or activities you will use to teach this topic to the following students in your class.

- Visual Learners _____

_____

_____

- Auditory Learners _____

_____

_____

- Kinesthetic/Tactile Learners _____

_____

_____

- Limited English Proficient (Identify level of English proficiency) _____

_____

_____

- Learners with Disabilities (Identify ESE classification for each student)

  _____

  _____

  _____

- Learners with 504 Plans _____

  _____

  _____

- Learners who Master Concepts Quickly _____

  _____

  _____

- Learners who Need Additional Practice and Instruction to Master Concepts

  _____

  _____

  _____

ACTIVITY G

IDENTIFYING GAPS IN SUBJECT MATTER KNOWLEDGE (FEAP 3)

The purpose of this activity is to identify gaps in your students' prior knowledge of the subject matter.

Directions: Complete Part 1 of this activity before teaching your lesson. After you have taught the lesson, complete Part 2.

Part 1:

1. What prior knowledge must your students have to understand the lesson you are preparing to teach?

_____

_____

_____

_____

2. List questions you can ask your students to assess their prior knowledge.

- _____

- _____

- _____

- _____

3. Do your students have the prior knowledge necessary for the lesson? What evidence do you have?

_____

_____

_____

_____

4. What preconceptions do your students have?

_____

_____

_____

_____

5. How will you modify instruction to address these preconceptions?

_____

_____

_____

Part 2:

1. What formative assessment did you use during your lesson to identify student mastery of the lesson's objectives?

_____

_____

_____

2. Did you identify any student misconceptions? If so, what are they? How will you clarify these misconceptions?

_____

_____

_____

ACTIVITY H

PROVIDING STUDENT FEEDBACK (FEAP 3)

Directions: Record a lesson you are teaching. Analyze your communication skills by answering the following questions.

1. Identify a time when you provided <u>immediate</u> and <u>specific</u> academic feedback to a student.

   _____

   _____

2. What did you say to support and encourage the student?

   _____

   _____

3. Identify a time when you used student feedback to identify instructional needs.

   _____

   _____

4. Based on the student feedback, how did you adjust your instruction?

   _____

   _____

ACTIVITY I

LEARNING WORDS WITH PICTURES (FEAP 3)

The purpose of this vocabulary activity is for each member of the cooperative learning group to be able to define all content vocabulary words at a 90% mastery or higher.

Teacher Tasks:
1. Select content vocabulary to be learned and social skills to be demonstrated.
2. Divide students into groups of 2, 3, or 4 depending on the number of vocabulary words you have selected and the number of students in your class.
3. Give each team markers and crayons and one 4x6 index card for each vocabulary word.
4. Select the time students will have to create images and teach words to each other.
5. Monitor the cooperative learning activity by checking the completion of the task and demonstration of the social skills selected (eye contact, taking turns, coming to consensus, etc.).
6. Conduct group processing/reflection.
7. Administer vocabulary test.

Cooperative Group Tasks:
1. The team will receive a list of the content vocabulary words and should divide the number of words evenly among members of the group.
2. Each team member will use index cards to illustrate the meaning of the words they are given. The illustration should go on one side of the card and the word on the other side. Each member must be able to explain to the group why his/her illustration depicts the meaning of the vocabulary word given.
3. Each member is responsible for teaching the other members of the group the vocabulary until all members can accurately define the words in the time allotted.
4. Students will be given 3 minutes to group process, discussing the effectiveness of their teamwork.
5. Each student will individually take the vocabulary test.
6. If all members of the group score 90% mastery or higher, all members will earn additional credit for active participation in the learning process.

RESOURCES

Anderson, L.W., & Krathwohl (Eds.). (2001). *A taxonomy for learning, teaching, and assessing: A revision of Bloom's Taxonomy of Educational Objectives*. New York: Longman.

Black, S. (2005). Teaching students to think critically. *The Education Digest*, 70(6), 42-7.

Brookhart, S. M. (2007). Feedback that fits. *Educational Leadership*, 65(4), 54-59.

Carr, K. (1988). How can we teach critical thinking? *Childhood Education*, 69-73.

Danielson, C. (2007, 2nd edition). *Enhancing professional practice: A framework for teaching.* Alexandria, VA: Association for Supervision and Curriculum Development.

Davis, B. G. (1993). *Tools for teaching*. San Francisco, CA: Jossey-Bass Publishers.

Domains: Knowledge base of the Florida Performance Measurement System. (2002). [Third Revised Edition]. Retrieved August 6, 2010, from http://www.duvalschools.org/newteachers/FPMS/FPMS%20Domain%20-%20CD%20Version.pdf

Donovan, M. S. & Bransford, J. D. (Ed.). (2005). *How students learn: History, mathematics, and science in the classroom*. Washington, DC: National Academies Press.

Florida Department of Education. (2010). *6A-5.065-The Educator Accomplished Practices as approved by the State Board of Education on December 17, 2010.* Retrieved December 21, 2010, from http://www.fldoe.org/profdev/FEAPSRevisions/

Joyce, B. & Weil, M. (1986). *Models of teaching.* Englewood Cliffs, NJ: Prentice Hall, Inc.

Marzano, R. (2009). Setting the record straight on "high-yield" strategies. *Phi Delta Kappan*, 91(1), 30-37.

Marzano, R. (2003). *What works in schools: translating research into action*. Alexandria, VA: ASCD.

Marzano, R. and Pickering, D. (2005). *Building academic vocabulary: Teacher's manual.* Alexandria, VA: ASCD.

Marzano, R., Pickering, J. & Pollock, J. (2001). *Classroom instruction that works,* Alexandria, VA: ASCD.

McCarthy, P. (1992). *Common teaching methods*. Retrieved May 5, 2010, from http://honolulu.hawaii.edu/intranet/committees/FacDevCom/guidebk/teachtip/comteach.htm

Public Consulting Group's Center for Resource Management, Initials. (2007). *Content area literacy guide* [CCSSO's Secondary School Redesign Project]. (Component of CCSSO's Adolescent Literacy Toolkit), Retrieved November 21, 2010, from http://www.kentuckyliteracy.org/alcp/Toolkit%20Contents/CCSSO-Content%20Area%20Literacy%20Guide.pdf

Shulman, L. S. . (1986). Those who understand: Knowledge growth in teaching. *Educational Researcher, 15*(4), Retrieved from http://edr.sagepub.com/content/15/2/4 doi: 10.3102/0013189X015002004

Webb, N. (2005, November 17). *Alignment, depth of knowledge, & change*. Retrieved May 8, 2010, from http://facstaff.wcer.wisc.edu/normw/MIAMI%20FLORIDA%20FINAL%20slides%2011-15-05.pdf

(2010, January 3). *Instructional methods information*. Retrieved May 5, 2010, from http://www.adprima.com/teachmeth.htm

ASSESSMENT

The effective educator consistently:

- Analyzes and applies data from multiple assessments and measures to diagnose students' learning needs, informs instructions based on those needs, and drives the learning process
- Designs and aligns formative and summative assessments that match learning objectives and lead to mastery
- Uses a variety of assessment tools to monitor student progress, achievement and learning gains
- Modifies assessments and testing conditions to accommodate learning styles and varying levels of knowledge
- Shares the importance and outcomes of student assessment data with the student and the student's parent/caregiver
- Applies technology to organize and integrate assessment information

Florida Educator Accomplished Practice #4:

ASSESSMENT

DID YOU KNOW...

Introduction:
When most people think of assessment they think of the traditional Friday spelling quiz or end-of-the chapter test in Social Studies. While those tests are a part of traditional assessment, they are not the whole of assessment in the modern classroom.

Assessments impact student learning and determine the effectiveness of the teacher. When linked to state academic standards and benchmarks, they provide the teacher, the student's parents, and the school with a measurement of the student's skills and knowledge. Assessments, specifically standardized tests, provide an indication whether the student has learned the curriculum covered by the teacher. Analysis of the data can be an effective tool for driving instruction.

The primary reasons teachers assess students are to (1) diagnose their students' strengths and weaknesses and (2) monitor their progress. Effective teachers assess their students formally (tests, rubrics, portfolios, projects, etc.) and informally (observation, oral questions, etc.). By frequently assessing their students, teachers can monitor progress and identify content areas that need remediation.

Vocabulary:

accommodation – process in which existing mental structures are modified or new ones created as a result of experiences that cannot be assimilated

alternative assessment – assessment of learning in ways that are different from traditional paper-and-pencil objective testing, such as a portfolio, project, or self-assessment (See authentic assessment.)

assessment – the relatively neutral process of finding out what students have or have not learned as a result of instruction (See also evaluation.)

assessment accommodations – using alternate assessments for students with significant cognitive disabilities

authentic assessment – the use of evaluation procedures (usually portfolios and projects) that are highly compatible with the instructional objectives; also referred to as accurate, active, aligned, alternative, direct, and performance assessment

criterion-referenced assessment – assessment in which standards are established and behaviors are judged against the preset guidelines, rather than against the behaviors of others

database – a computerized collection of records, consolidated into a common pool, to provide data for one or more multiple uses; an example is Filemaker Pro

data-driven instruction – using data to monitor student progress and make specific instructional decisions by targeting the student's needs

differentiated accountability – creating a system for distinguishing between schools in need of intervention and those that are closer to meeting their goals for improving student achievement in reading and math; differentiated accountability must address the four core principles of the No Child Left Behind Act (1) identifying schools in need of improvement, (2) defining the process for categorizing schools, (3) defining a system of interventions for schools in need, and (4) restructuring the lowest performing schools

evaluation – like assessment but includes making sense out of the assessment results, usually based on criteria or a rubric; evaluation is more subjective than is assessment

measurement – the process of collecting and interpreting data

norm referenced test – assessment that compares a student's skills to others in the same age group

performance assessment – students are evaluated on how well they perform a task

portfolio assessment – an alternative approach to evaluation that assembles representative samples of a student's work over time as a basis for assessment

post-assessment – assessment given to measure what students know after instruction has been delivered

pre-assessment – diagnostic assessment of what students know or think they know prior to the instruction

reliability – in measurement, the consistency with which an item or instrument is measured over time

rubric – an outline of the criteria used to assess a student's work

spreadsheet – the computer equivalent of a paper ledger sheet, consisting of a grid made from columns and rows; can be used for calculations; an example is Excel

storage device – a device for recording information (data)

summative assessment – assessment of learning after instruction is completed to determine mastery of competencies and/or skills (chapter tests, unit tests, and mid-term/final)

validity – in measurement, the degree to which an item or instrument measures that which it is intended to measure

WHY WE KNOW...

Research:

Before teachers assess students, they must decide which type of assessment to use and how often to assess the students. Procedures also need to be in place for students who were absent the day of the assessment.

TESTS AS ASSESSMENTS

Length of Test

When writing a test, teachers must keep in mind the length of time it will take the students to complete the assessment. Use the following chart as a guide.

TYPE OF QUESTION	TIME PER ITEM
Matching	1 minute
Multiple Choice	1 minute
Completion	1 minute
Identification	2-3 minutes
Short Explanation	2-3 minutes
Essay	10 + minutes

Types of Test Items

Teachers must also decide on the type of questions to include on the test. The 12 question types are listed below with an example for each.

Arrangement—items are arranged in a specific order, tests knowledge of sequence and order.

> *Place these U.S. presidents in order from the earliest to the most recent: Washington, Reagan, Ford, Lincoln*

Completion Drawing—student completes a drawing, tests knowledge of a concept

Complete filling in this circle so that the colored-in area represents 75% of the area of the circle.

Completion Statement or Fill-in—incomplete sentence is presented and student completes it by filling in the blank space; tests recall

A _____ is a word that names a person, place, or thing.

Corrections—sentences are completed with italicized or underlined words that can be changed to make the sentences correct; tests recall

Astronomy is the study of <u>astronauts</u>.

Essay—a question or problem is presented and student composes a response; good for testing critical thinking

Compare and contrast the political platforms of the Republican and Democratic parties during the election of 1968.

Grouping—several items are presented and students select those that are in some way connected; tests conceptual knowledge (be ready for students who use alternative reasons for grouping)

Group the following words by the parts of speech they represent: noun, verb, adjective, or adverb.

big	*soon*	*hot*	*pig*
running	*pencil*	*now*	*smelly*
girl	*picture*	*sandy*	*under*
tall	*walker*	*house*	*very*

Matching—match related items from a list of numbered items; tests recall or concepts (must have one more item in Column B than in Column A to prevent guessing)

Column A	Column B
__ Mexico	a. Continent
__ Pacific	b. Country
__ Africa	c. Ocean
__ Cairo	d. City
	e. Sea

Identification—the "unknown" is identified by name or some other criterion; tests recall

Identify the parts of the microscope indicated by arrows.

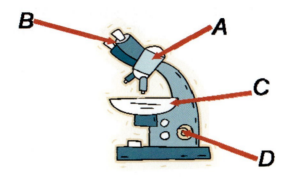

Multiple Choice—similar to completion but choices are presented; can be written to test higher-level knowledge; avoid using "all of the above" and "none of the above" as choices

Which of the following was a <u>direct</u> result of the Homestead Act?
a. Southern plantation owners moved West.
b. Large cattle ranchers gained control of water resources.
c. Gold and silver miners destroyed the land.
d. The Greenback Party rose to prominence.

Performance—given specific conditions, the student accomplishes an act; encourages creativity

I will call each of you to the front of the class to play a song for me. I will grade you on timing and interpretation.

Short Explanation—similar to essay but requires shorter answer; tests knowledge of concepts

Explain why Washington decided not to run for a third term.

True/False—students judge a statement as being true or false; student has a 50% chance of being correct; avoid tricky statements

____ *½ equals 50%*

Level of Questions

Teachers should write test items that vary in difficulty—from simple recall to higher order thinking. Teachers who place critical thinking questions on tests are requiring their students to apply, analyze, synthesize, and evaluate information instead of just remembering facts.

THE TESTING PROCESS

There are three parts of every test: (1) preparing the students for the test, (2) administering the test, and (3) providing students with feedback on their test results.

Preparing Students

When preparing students for a test, teachers need to orient the students to the test. Explain to the students how the results will be used and why the test is relevant. Teachers must also provide the students with a study guide, review the study guide with the students, and inform them of the types of questions (multiple choice, matching, etc.) that will be on the test. Test questions should only be based on curriculum standards/ teacher objectives that were taught in the lessons preceding the test. Tests should not be constructed to trick the students but to assess how well they mastered the objectives taught.

Administering the Test

Teachers are responsible for controlling the physical setting during the test. This includes lighting, temperature, and the seating of students. By making positive statements prior to the test, teachers can encourage students to do their best.

While students are taking the test, the teacher needs to monitor the classroom. This includes frequently walking around the room, letting the students know the teacher is aware of what they are doing. Since anxiety and cheating are related, students who are well prepared for the test are less likely to cheat. To discourage cheating, many teachers prepare different sets of the same test.

What does a teacher do if a student is caught cheating? Never embarrass the student by making accusations during the test. Quietly speak to the student after the test and follow the school's policy for cheating.

Test Feedback

After the teacher has graded the test, it is important to review the test results, make positive comments, and provide reasons for the answers. This can be done by setting time aside to identify common errors made by students and reviewing the correct responses. If there is no feedback as to the correct answer, students will repeat their mistakes on future assessments.

PERFORMANCE ASSESSMENTS

Assessments should be authentic, measureable, and linked to the objectives of the lesson. Traditional assessments used by teachers have been worksheets, homework, quizzes, and tests. Although these types of assessments are important, teachers should also utilize performance assessments to monitor student achievement.

Portfolios as Assessments

A portfolio is a collection of student work that shows evidence of the student's efforts, progress, and achievement in the class. The following are guidelines for teachers who decide to use portfolios as assessment tools.

- Make sure your students "own" their portfolios.
- Decide on the kind of work samples they should collect.
- Work samples need to be placed in a notebook or container.
- Identify criteria to evaluate all work samples.
- Require students to evaluate their own work samples.
- Schedule and conduct portfolio conferences with students.
- Make sure parents understand the portfolio assessment process. The portfolio samples are to be created by the student, not the parents.

Digital Portfolios

A digital portfolio, also known as an e-portfolio, is a collection of electronic evidence used to demonstrate a student's record of achievement. A portfolio may include text, images, web pages, and electronic versions of the student's work products.

Rubrics as Assessment Tools

Rubrics are an objective tool used to assess projects, presentations, reports, and other classroom assignments. Since the criteria for assessment are clearly defined in a rubric, along with the competencies needed to achieve a certain score at each level, the students have a clear understanding of the skills they must demonstrate. When creating a rubric, teachers should remember to:

- identify what is being assessed (content? skill?),
- list the criteria for what the best products will look like,
- list what will be totally unacceptable,
- decide what the in-between products will look like,
- keep the rubric brief and inclusive,
- review the rubric with students, and
- if possible, share past examples of good and bad work with students.

Difference Between Analytic and Holistic Rubrics

Analytic rubrics identify and assess components of a finished product. An example of an analytic rubric appears below.

Criteria	Exceeds Expectations 3	Meets Expectations 2	Does Not Meet Expectations 1
Plot	Plot is fully developed	Part of plot is missing	Plot is not addressed
Setting ("When" and "Where")	"When" and "Where" are fully addressed	One section of the setting is missing	Neither section of the setting is addressed
Characters	Characters are fully developed with great detail	Characters are developed in minor detail	There is no character development
Written Presentation	No grammar or spelling errors	1-5 grammar or spelling errors	More than 5 grammar or spelling errors

Holistic rubrics assess student work as a whole. An example of a holistic rubric appears below.

4 – The plot, setting and characters are fully developed. There are no grammar or spelling errors.
3 – Most of the plot, setting and characters are developed with some criteria being more developed than others are. There are no grammar or spelling errors.
2 – A few parts of the story are developed but not in much detail. There are grammar or spelling errors.
1 – Parts of the story are not addressed. There are grammar or spelling errors.

Neither type of rubric is better than the other. When deciding which type of rubric to use, teachers should take into account the age of the student being taught. Several sites on the Internet provide teachers with rubrics that can be easily adapted to meet the needs of their students.

Other Methods for Assessing Students

Effective teachers continually monitor student progress and achievement. Providing written and verbal comments can improve student learning. Items that should be assessed include:

- oral reports,
- responses to oral questions asked by the teacher,
- what a student writes,
- worksheets,
- homework,
- reports,
- projects,
- posters,
- oral presentations,
- group work products,
- peer evaluations,
- participation in class discussions, and
- demonstrations.

Identifying Student Needs by Interpreting Data

Pre-tests and data from previously administered norm referenced tests (NRT) can help teachers determine what their students already know and are capable of doing. Teachers can then identify the standards/benchmarks the students are lacking and create instructional activities to focus on their needs. If, by chance, teachers find a few students do not need any remediation, then the focus should be on creating enrichment activities for those students.

THE ASSESSMENT CYCLE

The assessment cycle is an effective tool for improving instruction. It consists of (1) assessing the students, (2) collecting data, (3) analyzing the data, (4) making instructional decisions, (5) delivering instruction, and (6) re-assessment of the students. The steps to follow when using the assessment cycle are as follows:

> **Step 1**: Assessment – Give a pre-test to determine what your students know.

> **Step 2**: Data Collection – What are the scores on the pre-test?

> **Step 3**: Aggregation of Data – What are the results? (item analysis, product analysis) By utilizing this step, teachers can identify poor test items. These items can then be corrected or eliminated from the post-assessment.

> **Step 4**: Display of Data – What does the data look like? (tables, bar graphs)

> **Step 5**: Analysis of Data – What do you see when you analyze the data?

> **Step 6**: Instructional Decisions – How will what you see affect what you will teach?

> **Step 7**: Instruction – What methods of instruction will you use to impact student learning?

> **Step 8**: Reassessment – Give a post-test to determine what your students learned. What was learned? Who learned it? What still needs to be learned? If it was not learned, why not? How will you remediate students who have not mastered the concepts or skills? How will you provide enrichment activities for students who have achieved mastery?

ASSESSMENT ACCOMMODATIONS

Assessment accommodations for **ESE students** include:

- changes in the way assessment is presented based on the student's IEP (Braille, sign language, visual enhancement);
- changes in the way the student responds to the assessment based on the student's IEP (signed response, verbal response, use of an assistive technology device);
- changes in scheduling of the assessment (allowing frequent breaks or more time to complete the assessment); and
- changes in the environment (taking the assessment in a smaller group or alone).

Assessment accommodations for **LEP students** include:

- giving the student additional time to complete the assessment,
- providing a dictionary (English-to-heritage language and heritage language-to-English), and
- changing the location to a room with other LEP students or having a heritage language teacher administer the assessment.

WHAT YOU NEED TO KNOW...

The teacher has the responsibility to collect, analyze, and use assessment data on a daily basis. Formative assessments such as one-on-one questioning and short quizzes occur during instruction. Results are provided instantly and allow teachers to adjust their instruction as needed.

Summative assessments such as unit tests and mid-terms occur at the end of a unit of instruction. Because assessment results are not instantaneous, these tests cannot guide daily instruction and are more often used as a basis for giving student grades.

Teachers must remember that assessment data is confidential and should only be shared with the student's parents and school staff (other teachers, counselors, support staff). Sharing student information, as described in the Family Educational Rights and Privacy Act (FERPA), requires permission from the parents or student, if over the age of 18 (U.S. Department of Education, n.d.).

DATA-DRIVEN INSTRUCTION

Data–driven instruction is using data to monitor student progress, make instructional decisions, and target student needs. There are many ways teachers can use data to improve instruction. Although district-wide assessments and formal classroom assessments (tests, worksheets) are the most common methods for gathering data, teachers must not forget using informal data such as conversations with other teachers who are working with the same students.

Eight-Step Instructional Process

The Eight-Step Instructional Process was developed in Brazosport Independent School District in Brazoria County, Texas, for the purpose of improving student achievement on assessments (Anderson, n.d.). The steps are listed below.

- Disaggregation of Test Scores—school analyzes class and individual test scores to identify strengths and needs of students
- Develop Timeline of Skills and Topics to be Taught—school creates a campus timeline for the instruction of standards and benchmarks
- Deliver Instructional Focus—teachers focus on benchmarks for a certain amount of time
- Administer Assessment—teachers assess student mastery of benchmarks
- Tutorials—teachers tutor students who do not reach mastery on benchmarks
- Enrichment—teachers provide enrichment to those who mastered the benchmarks
- Provide Ongoing Maintenance—teachers continuously review standards throughout the school year
- Monitoring—instructional leaders visit classrooms to monitor progress

LET IT SHOW!

Below is a list of different methods you can use to demonstrate your accomplishment of **FEAP #4: ASSESSMENT**.

(a) Analyzes and applies data from multiple assessments and measures to diagnose students' learning needs, informs instructions based on those needs, and drives the learning process

▶ Develop an Assessment Cycle for every unit of study. Use the data from the pre-assessment to drive instruction and the post-assessment to determine the remediation and enrichment required for students.

▶ Create a Pre-Test: Demonstrate your ability to assess your students by creating a pre-test for the first day of school or for the first day of a unit you are planning to teach. Analyze the data results and create lesson plans that address the needs of your students.

▶ Identify LEP Strategies: Identify your LEP students and their classifications. Identify the strategies you can use to improve their academic achievement in reading, writing, listening, and speaking.

(b) Designs and aligns formative and summative assessments that match learning objectives and lead to mastery

▶ Research Non-traditional types of Formative and Summative Assessments: Use the Internet, district, or other teacher resources to identify non-traditional formative and summative assessments strategies. Determine the best options for assessing mastery of learning in your curriculum.

▶ Create a Test: Create a test that has the majority of the questions at the Comprehension, Application, Analysis, Synthesis, and Evaluation levels.

▶ Create a Formative Assessment: Create questions to be asked during the lesson to test mastery of the lesson's objectives.

(c) Uses a variety of assessment tools to monitor student progress, achievement and learning gains

▶ Use Alternative Assessments: Demonstrate your ability to use alternative assessments such as student portfolios and group reports.

▶ Use Student Portfolios: Use portfolios to monitor the development of your students.

(d) Modifies assessments and testing conditions to accommodate learning styles and varying levels of knowledge

▶ Use a Learning Style Inventory: Select specific assessment tools that address the needs of visual, auditory, and kinesthetic learners.

▶ Research and/or Create Assessment Tools: Using Howard Gardner's theory of Multiple Intelligences, develop traditional and non-traditional assessment instruments or activities.

▶ Create a Project: Have your students create a project that assesses your students' mastery of the subject area content. Use a rubric to grade the project. Consider giving a group grade and individual grades.

(e) Shares the importance and outcomes of student assessment data with the student and the student's parent/caregiver

▶ Goal Management: Teach students how to set goals, self–assess, and chart progress.

▶ Parent/Student/Teacher Conference: During a meeting with a student and the student's parents, review the student's grades on assessments in your class. Explain how the grades reflect achievement of the subject material.

(f) Applies technology to organize and integrate assessment information

▶ Use Technology: Use school/district software to review assessment data and identify student needs.

ACTIVITY OVERVIEW FOR DEMONSTRATING PROFICIENCY IN
FEAP #4: ASSESSMENT

(a) Analyzes and applies data from multiple assessments and measures to diagnose students' learning needs, informs instructions based on those needs, and drives the learning process

> **Activity A: ASSESSMENT CYCLE ANALYSIS**

(b) Designs and aligns formative and summative assessments that match learning objectives and lead to mastery

> **Activity B: CREATING A RUBRIC**
> **Activity C: CREATING TEST ITEMS**

(c) Uses a variety of assessment tools to monitor student progress, achievement and learning gains

> **Activity D: DIGITAL PORTFOLIO**

(d) Modifies assessments and testing conditions to accommodate learning styles and varying levels of knowledge

> **Activity E: REFLECTION ON STUDENT ASSESSMENT**

(e) Shares the importance and outcomes of student assessment data with the student and the student's parent/caregiver

> **Activity F: ASSESSMENT OUTCOMES**

(f) Applies technology to organize and integrate assessment information

> **Activity A: ASSESSMENT CYCLE ANALYSIS**

ACTIVITY A

ASSESSMENT CYCLE ANALYSIS (FEAP 4)

The purpose of this activity is to provide you with an opportunity to create a pre- and post-assessment, review and analyze the data, and reflect on the results.

Part 1: Create a five-question pre-test (short answer or fill-in-the-blank only) based on what you plan to teach your students. Administer the pre-test to your students. Grade the pre-tests.

Part 2: Using an Excel worksheet, create a data table displaying class and individual student scores for each question. Create bar graphs to represent the data. What does each student know? What does each student need to know? An example of a table is provided below.

Individual Student Data

Student Identifier	Question 1 (Topic/ Objective)	Question 2 (Topic/ Objective)	Question 3 (Topic/ Objective)	Question 4 (Topic/ Objective)	Question 5 (Topic/ Objective)
Student 1					
Student 2					
Total percent correct					

Part 3: Analyze your test questions. Are they valid questions? Review the questions in which fewer than 50% of the students answered correctly. Look for patterns of responses among the highest achievers, lowest achievers, and linguistically and culturally diverse students. Do the patterns of responses indicate a need for revision of the item? Review questions for validity, reliability, bias, and scoring errors. An example of a three-column *Item Analysis* table showing the proportion of students correctly answering each item and your comments about the items is provided.

Item Analysis

Number of Students Taking Test: _____

Item #	% of Students Correct	Analysis of Items (items with 50%+ incorrect)
1		
2		
3		
4		
5		

Part 4: Based on your analysis of the pre-test data, align your lesson objectives to teach your class the information you assessed in the pre-test. After the lesson, administer the same test again (post-test) to your students. Grade the tests.

Part 5: Using the *Individual Student Data* table provided in this activity, analyze class and individual student scores for each question. Create bar graphs to represent the data. What did each student learn? What does each student still need to learn?

Part 6: Reflect on the effectiveness of your lesson plan. How will you remediate the students who did not learn?

Part 7: Reflect on the test and the lesson. Did the test evaluate the lesson objectives? How will you modify your lesson the next time you teach it?

ACTIVITY B

CREATING A RUBRIC (FEAP 4)

Part 1: Students will learn _____

_____

Example: (1) causes of the Civil War, (2) how the North & South felt about the causes, (3) alignment of the states during the war

Part 2: Create a project to help students learn the material you identified in Part 1.

Description of Project:

_____

_____

_____

_____

Example: Students will create a poster. On one side of the poster, the students will identify the causes of the Civil War and how the North & South felt about the causes. On the other side of the poster, the students will draw a map of the United States, identifying alignment of the Northern & Southern states.

Part 3: Identify three or four Criteria you will use to assess the project. You will place these criteria on the blank rubric form provided. (Each criterion should have only 1-3 words.)

        Criterion 1: _____

        Criterion 2: _____

        Criterion 3: _____

        Criterion 4: _____

Example: Criterion 1 = Neatness; Criterion 2 = Causes of War; Criterion 3 = States Map; Criterion 4 = Accuracy

Part 4: Identify the values for student performance.

1. What do you want to see in each of the criterion that will make the project "Excellent"? Be specific. Enter this information in the **Advanced** column.
2. What will you consider to be "Average" in each of the criterion? Enter this information in the **Proficient** column.
3. What will you consider to be "Below Average" in each of the criterion? Enter this information in the **Basic** column.

BASIC RUBRIC

CRITERIA	ADVANCED (3 PTS)	PROFICIENT (2 PTS)	BASIC (1 PT) OR MISSING (0 PTS)

ACTIVITY C

CREATING TEST ITEMS (FEAP 4)

Write nine test questions using at least eight different types of questions discussed in this chapter. Use the following levels of the New Blooms Taxonomy to write your questions:

▶ Apply
▶ Analyze
▶ Evaluate
▶ Create

1. Type of Question: _____

   Blooms Level of Question: _____

   Question: _____

   _____

2. Type of Question: _____

   Blooms Level of Question: _____

   Question: _____

   _____

3. Type of Question: _____

   Blooms Level of Question: _____

   Question: _____

   _____

4. Type of Question: _____

   Blooms Level of Question: _____

   Question: _____

   _____

5. Type of Question: _____

   Blooms Level of Question: _____

   Question: _____

   _____

6. Type of Question: _____

   Blooms Level of Question: _____

   Question: _____

   _____

7. Type of Question: _____

   Blooms Level of Question: _____

   Question: _____

   _____

8. Type of Question: _____

   Blooms Level of Question: _____

   Question: _____

   _____

9. Type of Question: _____

   Blooms Level of Question: _____

   Question: _____

   _____

ACTIVITY D

DIGITAL PORTFOLIO (FEAP 4)

The purpose of this activity is to create a digital portfolio that demonstrates your ability to:
- create a lesson plan,
- create a classroom management plan,
- create an assessment tool that requires students to use critical thinking skills,
- create engaging instructional activities that facilitate learning,
- analyze student data and make instructional decisions based on that data,
- differentiate instruction based on the needs of your students, and
- communicate with parents and other school stakeholders.

ACTIVITY E

REFLECTION ON STUDENT ASSESSMENT (FEAP 4)

Review an assessment in which your students performed below expectation. Answer the following:

1. Did the <u>testing conditions</u> (seating arrangements, climate control, lighting, disruptions, noise, length of assessment, etc.) contribute to the students' poor performance? Why or why not?

    _____

    _____

    _____

    _____

    If testing conditions affected assessment results, how will you modify the conditions for the next assessment?

    _____

    _____

    _____

    _____

2. Did the assessment address the various learning styles and level of knowledge of your students?

    _____

    If you answered "yes," explain how you made the accommodations and attach a copy of the assessment.

    If you answered "no," modify the assessment to make accommodations and attach a copy of the revised assessment.

ACTIVITY F

ASSESSMENT OUTCOMES (FEAP 4)

Directions: Answer the questions below to demonstrate how you have shared information about assessments with your students and their parents.

Class Assessments: (Type) _____

1. How did you explain the importance of the assessment(s) to your students?

   _____

   _____

2. How did you share the assessment results with the parents of your students?

   _____

   _____

District Assessments: (Type) _____

1. How did you explain the importance of the assessment(s) to your students?

   _____

   _____

2. How did you share the assessment results with the parents of your students?

   _____

   _____

State Assessments: (Type) _____

1. How did you explain the importance of the assessment(s) to your students?

   _____

   _____

2. How did you share the assessment results with the parents of your students?

   _____

   _____

RESOURCES

Anderson, G. (n.d.). *Brazosport Independent School District: Implementation of the quality agenda to ensure excellence and equity for all students.* Retrieved March 3, 2010, from http://assets.pearsonschool.com/asset_mgr/legacy/200727/2001_05Anderson_407_1.pdf

Chapman, C. & King, R. (2005). Differentiated assessment *strategies: One tool doesn't fit all.* Thousand Oaks, CA: Corwin Press, Inc.

Cross, L. D., Murray, S. S., Pullease, B. G. & Targoff, H. W. (2008). *Setting the stage for effective teaching practices: A research & resource guide.* Boston, MA: Pearson, Allyn & Bacon.

Domains: Knowledge base of the Florida Performance Measurement System. (2002). [Third Revised Edition]. Retrieved August 6, 2010, from http://www.duvalschools.org/newteachers/FPMS/FPMS%20Domain%20-%20CD%20Version.pdf

Florida Department of Education. (2010). *6A-5.065-The Educator Accomplished Practices as approved by the State Board of Education on December 17, 2010.* Retrieved December 21, 2010, from http://www.fldoe.org/profdev/FEAPSRevisions/

Rudner, L., & Schafer, W. (2002). *What teachers need to know about assessment.* Washington, D.C.: National Education Association.

U.S. Department of Education. (n.d.). *Family Educational Rights and Privacy Act (FERPA).* Retrieved April 12, 2010, from http://www.ed.gov/policy/gen/guid/fpco/ferpa/index.html

U.S. Department of Education (2004, September 19). *Testing for results: Helping families, schools and communities understand and improve student achievement.* Retrieved April 13, 2010, from http://www.ed.gov/nclb/accountability/ayp/testingforresults.html?exp=5

CONTINUOUS IMPROVEMENT, RESPONSIBILITY AND ETHICS

FLORIDA EDUCATOR ACCOMPLISHED PRACTICES

- #5: Continuous Professional Improvement
- #6: Professional Responsibility and Ethical Conduct

CONTINUOUS PROFESSIONAL IMPROVEMENT

The effective educator consistently:

- **Designs purposeful professional goals to strengthen the effectiveness of instruction based on students' needs**
- **Examines and uses data-informed research to improve instruction and student achievement**
- **Collaborates with the home, school and larger communities to foster communication and to support student learning and continuous improvement**
- **Engages in targeted professional growth opportunities and reflective practices, both independently and in collaboration with colleagues**
- **Implements knowledge and skills learned in professional development in the teaching and learning process**

Florida Educator Accomplished Practice #5:

CONTINUOUS PROFESSIONAL IMPROVEMENT

DID YOU KNOW...

Introduction:
Continuous improvement, a career-long commitment for teachers, is the process of improving teacher competencies. Research shows that when teachers commit to continuous improvement, student achievement increases.

On January 8, 2002, the No Child Left Behind (NCLB) bill was signed into law. Calling for a quality education for all students, the law specifically states that all teachers in core classrooms must be "highly qualified" (U.S. Department of Education, 2004).

To be considered highly qualified, a teacher must have a bachelor's degree, state certification, and knowledge of the subject taught. Teachers in middle/junior high and high school must prove they know the subject they teach by majoring in the subject at the college level and passing a state-developed test. In addition to being highly qualified when entering the teaching profession, teachers must constantly update their skills to meet the needs of their students.

Vocabulary:

clinical education training – professional development for teachers in the areas of performance standards, diagnosis and feedback on professional performance, diagnosis and feedback on student performance, and implementation of professional development plans

developing teacher – a pre-service or new teacher

faculty learning communities – a small group of faculty members working collaboratively to increase their professional knowledge and skills

in-service or professional development workshops – workshops offered by school districts to full-time instructional staff employed in that district

NCLB – No Child Left Behind law that called for all teachers to be highly qualified in the subject(s) they teach

professional associations – organizations that offer professional support and development for teachers; examples are the National Education Association, the Association of American Educators, and associations specific to levels and subject areas

professional development plan – a plan that identifies the educator's deficiencies; needed for improvement to stay employed as a productive teacher

professional growth plan – a plan that identifies the educator's explicit learning goals and has as its overall goal the improvement of student learning

professional staff development – formal or informal training for educators; can range from a single workshop to a college-level course

WHY WE KNOW…

Research

Teachers can begin their path to continuous improvement in several ways. They can develop professional growth plans, reflect on their own practices, examine and use findings from research, participate in action research, or seek assistance from a colleague.

PROFESSIONAL DEVELOPMENT

Profession Growth Plans

Every Florida teacher completes a Professional Growth Plan annually, pursuant to Florida Statute 1012.98(4b)(5). This plan must have as its overall goal the improvement of student learning that is specific to the needs of the students the teacher is assigned. The steps for developing a Professional Growth Plan are:

- identifying the academic needs of the students assigned to the teacher,
- identifying the teacher's staff development objectives to improve student learning, and
- measuring student improvement as a result of the staff development.

At the end of the school year, an evaluation component determines the effectiveness of the professional development plan.

Self-Reflection

Teachers can also improve their skills through self-reflection, a process of self-evaluation used to improve professional practices. Effective teachers reflect on what has taken place in a specific situation, identify options available, and make conscious choices on how to make a difference in the future. They must continually study their practices and concentrate on developing skills that help them become more effective.

Research / Action Research

Teachers who examine and use findings from research can transform their practice and become more effective classroom teachers. Teachers who become involved in action research with their colleagues participate in a collaborative activity in which they search for ways to improve instruction and increase student achievement.

Learning Communities

The goal of Learning Communities is to advance student learning by improving teacher skills. Learning Communities consist of teams of teachers who meet on a regular basis for the purpose of joint lesson planning, problem solving, reading and discussing articles, and inviting consultants to assist them in acquiring skills.

Colleagues

Teachers can enhance their skills by observing colleagues teach a lesson. After identifying effective teacher behaviors, they can integrate what they learned into their own classrooms. Teachers can also ask a trusted peer to observe their classrooms and offer suggestions for improvement.

WHAT YOU NEED TO KNOW...

Teachers in Florida are required to renew their teaching certificate every five years, during the validity of the professional certificate and prior to its expiration.

CERTIFICATION

To renew a certificate, Florida teachers can do one of the following:

- complete six semester hours of college credit from an accredited or approved institution, with a passing grade for each college course used for renewal; or
- complete 120 hours of appropriate in-service credit offered through their school district; or
- complete three semester hours of college credit from an accredited or approved institution, with a passing grade for each college course used for renewal, and 60 hours of appropriate in-service offered through their school district.

The following topics for college courses or in-service are appropriate for renewing a Professional Certificate:

- Content specific to the subject area(s)
- Methods or education strategies specific to the subject area(s)
- Methods of teaching reading and literacy skills acquisition
- Computer literacy, computer applications, and computer education
- Exceptional student education
- ESOL (English for Speakers of Other Languages)
- Drug abuse, child abuse and neglect, or student dropout prevention
- Training in:

  o **Content**—English, economics, mathematics, science, social sciences, foreign languages, humanities, global economy, technology, ecology, first aid, health, or safety

  o **Classroom Strategies**—cooperative learning, problem-solving skills, critical-thinking skills, classroom management, child development, collaboration techniques for working with families, social services, child guidance and counseling, teaching reading, or educational assessments, etc.

  o **School Administration Accountability**—instructional design, leadership skills, school and community relations, school finance, school facilities, school law, or school organization

- o **Vocational and Adult Education Accountability**—adult learning, principles of adult or vocational education, vocational education for students with special needs, or vocational guidance

The application for renewal and the appropriate fee must be submitted during the last year of the validity period of the certificate and prior to its expiration. All Florida Educator's Certificates validity periods begin July 1st and end June 30th ranging from three years to five years, depending on the type of certificate held. The Bureau of Educator Certification does renew applications after the expiration of the Professional Certificate (Florida Educator Certification Renewal Requirements, 2009). For current information on renewal of Professional Certificates, go to the website for Florida's Bureau of Educator Certification.

PARENT-TEACHER CONFERENCES

Communication between teachers and parents requires good listening techniques, tact, kindness, honesty, and empathy. In addition, parents often have important perspectives about their children that can help teachers. Parents and teachers working together with a common goal can improve student achievement.

When attending a parent-teacher conference, the teacher should use the sandwich technique—start and end the conference with positive comments about the child; get to the meat of the problem in the middle. It is helpful to initiate the conference pleasantly by starting with a positive comment such as, "Thank you for coming to this conference. I hope the two of us can create a successful team to support your child."

<u>**Tips for Making Parent Conferences Successful**</u>

- **Invite both parents** – Remember, though, that many students do not come from two-parent households.
- **Allow enough time for the conference** – 20-30 minutes is adequate time to meet and confer with parents.
- **Be ready for questions** – Parents are likely to ask questions such as:
  "Is my child working up to ability level?"
  "What type of grades is my child earning?"
  "Does my child misbehave in class?"
  "How often do you assign homework?"
  "Does my child need any assistance to improve grades?"
- **Have documentation** – Take your gradebook, attendance records, and samples of the student's work to the meeting.
- **Plan what you are going to say** – Give a review of the student's strengths and needs, as well as a proposed plan to assist the student.
- **The meeting** – Start the meeting by making a positive statement about the student's abilities or interests. Be specific in your comments and ask for the parents' opinions. Be sure to use non-threatening body language. Stress

collaboration by letting the parents know you want to work with them. Focus on solutions and end the meeting on a positive note. Always keep a record of the conference and notes on the topics discussed.

- **Confidentiality** – Remember, never discuss other students during the meeting.

Effective Teachers & Conferences

Pre-service teachers at Syracuse University's School of Education participated in a semester-long program in which they engaged in simulated parent-teacher conferences (Dotger & Sapon-Shevin, 2009). At the end of the program, participants learned that an effective teacher:

- listened well to the parents, regardless of the situation;
- made positive comments about the student along with constructive critiques;
- made the parents feel welcomed;
- carefully addressed all concerns of the parents;
- remained calm during conferences;
- made only realistic promises to the parents;
- offered the parent encouragement;
- listened to the ideas or suggestions of the parents; and
- was warm, enthusiastic and professional during the conference.

Facilitators of the Syracuse program also learned that:

- teachers and parents begin conferences from different perspectives,
- new teachers have difficulty identifying specific solutions to problems and often place the responsibility for the problem on the student,
- many new teachers were not well aware of bullying and harassment policies, and
- new teachers were sometimes overwhelmed by instructional demands of their jobs and frequently found it difficult resolving problems in social interactions.

OTHER COMMUNICATION WITH PARENTS

Communication with parents should not be limited to scheduled conferences that are arranged when something goes wrong. Teachers should make positive phone calls or send positive letters or notes to parents. Research shows that children do better in school when parents and teachers communicate often.

Electronic Communication

Teachers can communicate with students and parents through websites. Class websites can communicate homework, projects, and topics taught, as well as upcoming events. They are a great way to keep parents informed and connected to the school. Many school districts offer professional development workshops for teachers interested in learning to build websites with district-licensed programs.

Teachers frequently ask if it is appropriate to email or text their students (or former students) or to include them as "friends" on their social networking sites (MySpace, Facebook, or Twitter). Teachers should only communicate with students on official school email accounts or school web sites. Any communication, including telephone calls, should be limited to school matters. Personal communication could be considered inappropriate and unethical, and might lead to disciplinary action.

Parents often email teachers at the school's email address. When responding to parents, teachers must remain professional. Since email is a representation of the teacher, always use proper grammar and punctuation. Remember, email messages between parents and teachers are public documents.

Newsletters

Weekly or monthly newsletters are a positive and effective means of communicating with parents about the activities and skills being taught in the classroom. Newsletters can be delivered electronically or in paper form. Individual messages regarding specific students should never be expressed in the newsletters to all parents. Students may produce newsletters under the guidance of the teacher, as long as the newsletters have been proofread and are approved by the teacher or school administrator prior to distribution.

Open House

An Open House, also known as Back to School Night, is a perfect opportunity for parents to be welcomed into the school and classroom. This event allows the teacher to share the curriculum and classroom policies with parents so they can be supportive at home. The teacher should develop an Open House plan in accordance with school and district policies and expectations. The plan should include the following components.

- An overview of the curriculum—an outline for the entire year or semester, depending on length of course
- Expected student outcomes—including academic projects and assignments, examinations that will be administered, behavioral expectations (including rules and procedures)
- Grading scale and how student progress will be communicated—for example, mid-term progress reports, quarterly report cards, phone calls
- Homework and other policies
- Volunteer opportunities for parents/families to participate in classroom and/or school activities
- Ways in which parents/families can support and reinforce classroom goals, objectives, and standards (for example, provide a quiet location for the student to complete homework)
- Ways in which parents can contact the teacher
- Description of physical arrangement of the room for the Open House, including displays and student work
- Ways in which those not in attendance will receive the information presented in the Open House presentation

COMMUNICATION & CONFIDENTIALITY OF STUDENT RECORDS

Teachers must be very careful when disclosing information about students. Teachers cannot call out students' grades in class, nor can they post student lists with names of students and their respective grades indicated. To do so would be a violation of the 1974 Family Educational Rights and Privacy law.

The Family Educational Rights and Privacy Act is a federal law that protects the privacy of student education records. The law applies to all schools that receive funds from the U.S. Department of Education. The following are important aspects to the law that teachers must know. The term "eligible students" refers to students who are at least 18 years of age (U.S. Department of Education, n.d.).

- Parents or eligible students have the right to inspect and review the student's education records maintained by the school.
- Parents or eligible students have the right to request that a school correct records they believe to be inaccurate or misleading.
- Generally, schools must have written permission from the parent or eligible student in order to release any information from a student's education record. However, school officials with legitimate educational interest can review the records without consent.

LET IT SHOW!

Below is a list of different methods you can use to demonstrate your accomplishment of **FEAP #5: CONTINUOUS PROFESSIONAL IMPROVEMENT**.

(a) Designs purposeful professional goals to strengthen the effectiveness of instruction based on students' needs

▶ Complete a Professional Growth Plan: Identify the needs of your students. Then identify the professional development classes/workshops you can take to help you meet their needs.

▶ Join a Learning Community: Participate in a school learning community that discusses best practices related to student achievement in the areas of reading, writing, and critical thinking. Apply these best practices in your classroom.

(b) Examines and uses data-informed research to improve instruction and student achievement

▶ Review Your Lesson Plans: Review your lesson plans and identify the instructional strategies you most often use to deliver instruction. Identify new instructional strategies you can incorporate in your lessons.

▶ Participate in a Small Faculty Learning Community in Your School: Share experiences with other teachers in your school by participating in a small faculty learning community. Study and discuss innovative teaching strategies that improve student achievement.

▶ Participate in an Action-Research Project: Team with other teachers to develop an action–research project related to student achievement. Formulate a question, research strategies/methods, implement strategies/methods, collect and analyze data, and then reflect on the findings.

(c) Collaborates with the home, school and larger communities to foster communication and to support student learning and continuous improvement

▶ Write a Letter to Parents of Your Students: Demonstrate your ability to write a letter to parents of your students. Describe expectations for your students and homework policies. Identify times you are available for conferences and telephone calls.

▶ Create a Weekly Report Form: Demonstrate your ability to create a weekly report to communicate student achievement to parents.

▶ Communicate with Parents: Send a newsletter home to the parents of your students. Let them know what is being learned in class.

▶ Email a Parent: Email parents information on their child's progress in your class.

▶ Create a class newsletter: Highlight class activities and project/assignment due dates.

- ▶ Create a class website: Highlight school and class activities/topics and projects/assignments.
- ▶ Prepare for a Teacher-Parent Conference: Write questions you may have prior to the conference. Assemble copies of student work to share with the parent(s).
- ▶ Use a Telephone Log: Maintain a telephone log of calls made to parents.
- ▶ Communicate with Parents: Make it a point to start out the year on a positive note by calling a child's parent to make at least one positive comment.
- ▶ Review Your School's Improvement Plan: Meet with your colleagues to identify the academic needs of your students. Review your lesson plans to determine if you are addressing their needs. Adjust your lesson plans as needed.

(d) Engages in targeted professional growth opportunities and reflective practices, both independently and in collaboration with colleagues
- ▶ Attend a Professional Conference: Incorporate the strategies/methodologies you learned into your instruction.
- ▶ Attend Professional Staff Development: Locate the list of staff development opportunities offered by your district. Attend workshops that will help you improve your teaching skills.
- ▶ Take a college course or go to graduate school: Take a course in your content area or enhance/ learn a new teaching skill.
- ▶ Create a Professional Portfolio: Reflect on your best practices and select artifacts that demonstrate your professional growth and competencies in the classroom and school.

(e) Implements knowledge and skills learned in professional development in the teaching and learning process
- ▶ Pass a FTCE SAE Exam: Take and pass a Florida Teacher Certification Exam – Subject Area Exam in a content area.

ACTIVITY OVERVIEW FOR DEMONSTRATING PROFICIENCY IN

FEAP #5: CONTINUOUS PROFESSIONAL IMPROVEMENT

(a) Designs purposeful professional goals to strengthen the effectiveness of instruction based on students' needs

> **Activity B: PROFESSIONAL GROWTH PLAN RELATED TO STUDENT ACHIEVEMENT**
> **Activity D: TECHNOLOGY PROFICIENCY ASSESSMENT**

(b) Examines and uses data-informed research to improve instruction and student achievement

> **Activity F: ANECDOTAL RECORD**
> **Activity G: VIDEO ANALYSIS OF INSTRUCTION**

(c) Collaborates with the home, school and larger communities to foster communication and to support student learning and continuous improvement

> **Activity E: PARENT-TEACHER CONFERENCE ROLE PLAYING**
> **Activity H: OPEN HOUSE PRESENTATION**

(d) Engages in targeted professional growth opportunities and reflective practices, both independently and in collaboration with colleagues

> **Activity A: CONTINUOUS IMPROVEMENT CLASSROOM STRATEGIES & ASSESSMENT SURVEY**

(e) Implements knowledge and skills learned in professional development in the teaching and learning process

> **Activity C: LESSON PLAN SELF-REFLECTION**

ACTIVITY A

CONTINUOUS IMPROVEMENT CLASSROOM STRATEGIES & ASSESSMENT SURVEY (FEAP 5)

Complete this survey to help you identify areas in which you might need professional development.

O YES   O NO   1. I integrate technology into my classroom lessons.

O YES   O NO   2. I know how to analyze assessment data in order to identify the needs of my students.

O YES   O NO   3. I implement critical thinking strategies into my classroom activities.

O YES   O NO   4. My classroom can be described as a "well-oiled machine". My students are well behaved and are always on task.

O YES   O NO   5. I use various teaching strategies, including cooperative learning groups.

O YES   O NO   6. I use various assessment instruments.

O YES   O NO   7. My class activities meet the learning styles of all my students.

O YES   O NO   8. My lessons engage my students in the learning process.

O YES   O NO   9. I use resources other than the textbook.

O YES   O NO   10. I use graphic organizers to help my students learn.

Based on this survey, I need professional development in the area(s) of:

_____

_____

List in-service workshops, conferences, or college-level courses that are available for you to take for continuous improvement.

_____

ACTIVITY B

PROFESSIONAL GROWTH PLAN RELATED TO STUDENT ACHIEVEMENT (FEAP 5)

The purpose of a Professional Growth Plan is to increase achievement of your students. Complete this form to assist in the development of your plan.

Part 1:

Teacher Name: _____ Subject: _____ Grade ___

Benchmark/Standard Tested: _____

Specific Performance Data of Your Students:

Data Ranges	All Students		At-Risk Students		LEP Students		ESE Students	
	# of Students	% of Students	# of Students	% of Students	# of Students	% of Students	# of Students	% of Students
0-30%								
31-50%								
51-69%								
70-100%								
TOTALS								

Part 2:

1. What trends do you see in your data?

2. How did your At-Risk, LEP, and ESE students perform?

3. How are you presently assisting your students in the 0-30% range?

4. How are you presently assisting your students in the 31-50% range?

5. How will you move your students in the 51-69% range towards mastery?

Part 3:

1. Identify the needs of your students.

CATEGORY	NEEDS
0-30%	
31-50%	
51-69%	
70-100%	
At-Risk	
LEP	
ESE	

Part 4:

1. Develop a goal(s) to improve the achievement of your students. The goal(s) need(s) to be S.M.A.R.T. (specific, measureable, attainable, resources, and time).

2. Identify the professional development you need to assist your students in the achievement of the goal(s). (The professional development must be directly related to improved job performance that positively impacts student achievement.)

Part 5:

At the end of the year, reflect on the impact of your professional development on student achievement.

ACTIVITY C

LESSON PLAN SELF-REFLECTION (FEAP 5)

Directions: Complete this self-reflection focusing on:
    (1) the lesson you taught, and
    (2) how you demonstrated knowledge and skills learned in professional development throughout the lesson.

Lesson Content/Topic_____

Reflection:

1. Describe the part of the lesson you feel was the most effective for the students. Cite specific reasons for your feelings.

2. Describe the part of the lesson you feel was the least effective for the students. Cite specific reasons for your feelings.

3. What prior knowledge of your students told you the level of difficulty was appropriate?

4. What did you say or do that communicated high expectations to the students?

5. What effective classroom/behavioral management techniques did you use during the lesson?

6. Which presentation strategies/techniques were effective for this lesson? How do you know?

7. How will you help the students who did not demonstrate adequate comprehension of content and/or skill development?

8. How will you provide enrichment to students who mastered the content?

ACTIVITY D

TECHNOLOGY PROFICIENCY ASSESSMENT (FEAP 5)

Instructions: Complete each section of the assessment. Place an "**X**" in front of the statements that describe your skill level.

Basic Computer Operation

_____ I can use the computer to run a few specific, preloaded programs. It has little effect on either my work or home life. I am somewhat anxious I might damage the machine or its programs.

_____ I can setup my computer and peripheral devices, load software, print, and use most of the operating tools like the clipboard, scrapbook, clock, notepad, find command, help features, and trash can.

_____ I can run two programs simultaneously, and have several windows open at the same time. I can customize the look and sounds of my computer. I use shortcut techniques to work with multiple programs.

_____ I look for programs and techniques to maximize my operating system. I feel confident enough to teach others some basic operations.

File Management

_____ I can save/retrieve documents.

_____ I can create folders and move documents from one folder to another.

_____ I backup my files frequently.

_____ I regularly run a disk-optimizer on my hard drive.

_____ I can create a document in pdf format.

Word Processing

_____ I have never used word processing software.

_____ I occasionally use word processing software for simple documents that I know I will modify and use again.

_____ I use the word processing software for nearly all my written professional work. I can edit and spell check a document.

_____ I have advanced word processing skills. I can change the format of a document, use columns, create/edit templates, create tables, and import graphics.

Spreadsheet

_____ I have never used a spreadsheet.

_____ I understand the use of a spreadsheet and can navigate within one. I can create a simple spreadsheet that adds a column of numbers.

_____ I use a spreadsheet for several purposes. I use labels and built-in functions. I can change the format of the spreadsheets by changing column width and text style. I can also use the spreadsheet to make a simple graph or chart.

_____ I use advanced features such as cell references, formulas, and macros. I can import or export data.

Database

_____ I have never used a database.

_____ I understand the use of a database and can locate information within one that has been pre-made. I can add or delete data in a database.

_____ I use databases to collect and analyze data. I can create a simple database from scratch—defining fields and creating layouts. I can sort and print the information that is useful to me.

_____ I use advanced features of the database to create custom layouts and summations of numerical data. I can import and export data.

Graphics Use

_____ I can open, create, modify and place graphics into documents in order to help clarify or amplify my message.

_____ I can manipulate and interpret graphics using image-processing software (such as Photoshop) for the purpose of design.

Search Engines

_____ I can use a search engine for simple web navigation and research.

_____ I am able to create bookmarks.

_____ I can create my own web pages.

Email & Communication

_____ I can attach files to my email.

_____ I can create mailing lists and participate in on-line chats.

_____ I know how to save my email to folders on my desktop.

_____ I can create a calendar on my email system and send reminders of important meetings to all participants.

Presentations

_____ I can create simple presentations (e.g., PowerPoint).

_____ I can add graphics to my presentations.

_____ I can add animation, video, and sound to my presentations.

Hardware

_____ I can connect a printer to my computer.

_____ I can scan documents and create files of these documents.

_____ I can connect a laptop to an LCD projector or TV.

_____ I can use a flash drive to transfer data from one computer to another.

ACTIVITY E

PARENT-TEACHER CONFERENCE ROLE PLAYING (FEAP 5)

The purpose of this activity is to provide you with an opportunity to practice participating in a parent-teacher conference. Two participants are needed for each scenario below—one participant will play the role of the parent and the other participant will play the role of the teacher. The statements for each role will help you begin your conference.

Scenario 1

Teacher: Your son never turns in his work and is failing my class.

Parent: My son claims that he is failing because he does not understand the way you teach.

Scenario 2

Parent: My daughter is being bullied by another student in your class.

Teacher: *(Respond)*

Scenario 3

Teacher: Your daughter is always disrupting my class by talking and arguing with other students.

Parent: My daughter never had any problems until she had you as a teacher. She tells me that you are always picking on her.

Scenario 4

Teacher: Your son is having trouble concentrating in class. His grades are falling.

Parent: My husband and I are going through a divorce.

ACTIVITY F

ANECDOTAL RECORD (FEAP 5)

Teachers are frequently asked to make an anecdotal record on one of their students. An anecdotal record is a teacher's record of a student's social, emotional, physical, or cognitive development. In this activity, you will write an anecdotal record on a student in your class.

Student's Name: _____

Date: _____   Time: _____

    Comments on student's social interactions with classmates:

    Comments on student's emotional well-being:

    Comments on student's participation in instructional activities:

Date: _____   Time: _____

    Comments on student's social interactions with classmates:

    Comments on student's emotional well-being:

    Comments on student's participation in instructional activities:

Date: _____   Time: _____

    Comments on student's social interactions with classmates:

    Comments on student's emotional well-being:

    Comments on student's participation in instructional activities:

ACTIVITY G

VIDEO ANALYSIS OF INSTRUCTION (FEAP 5)

In this activity, you will videotape a lesson you are presenting to your class. After viewing the tape, answer the following questions.

1. Did you begin class on time? Why or why not?

2. Did your students know the purpose of the lesson? How did you relate the purpose to your class?

3. Were you aware of any students who were off task?

4. How did you keep students on task?

5. Were all students engaged in the activities?

6. What questions did you ask to check for understanding? Did the students respond correctly?

7. Did you ask a mix of lower and higher order questions?

8. How do you know the students learned the material?

9. How did you communicate your high expectations to the students?

10. Based on the videotape analysis, what were your strengths in this lesson? What were the areas you need to improve?

   Strengths:

   Improvement Needed:

ACTIVITY H

OPEN HOUSE PRESENTATION (FEAP 5)

Directions: Develop a PowerPoint or interactive whiteboard presentation for your Open House/Back-to-School Night. Incorporate all of the appropriate components listed below into your presentation.

- Introductory slide—introduce yourself and present your qualifications and teaching experience
- Beliefs and expectations for student performance—these may include academic projects, assignments, and behavioral expectations (including rules and procedures)
- Curriculum overview—overview of the course(s) for the year or semester, depending on the length of the course(s)
- Instructional strategies
- Daily routines
- Homework
- Grading practices—grading scale and how you will communicate student progress (mid-term progress reports, report cards, phone calls)
- Ways in which parents/families can support and reinforce classroom goals, objectives, and standards (for example, a quiet location for the student to complete homework)
- Volunteer opportunities for parents/families to participate in classroom and/or school activities
- Ways in which parents can reach you

RESOURCES

Ball, D. L. & Cohen, D. K. (1999). Developing practice, developing practitioners: Toward a practice-based theory of professional education. In G. Sykes and L. Darling-Hammond (Eds.), *Teaching as the learning profession: Handbook of policy and practice* (pp. 3-32). San Francisco: Jossey Bass.

Danielson, C. (2007, 2nd edition). *Enhancing professional practice: A framework for teaching.* Alexandria, VA: Association for Supervision and Curriculum Development.

Dotger, B., & Sapon-Shevin, M. (2009). But what do I say? *Educational Leadership*, 66(9), Retrieved March 18, 2010, from http://www.ascd.org/publications/educational_leadership/summer09/vol66/num09/But_What_Do_I_Say%C2%A2.aspx

Florida Department of Education. (2010). *6A-5.065-The Educator Accomplished Practices as approved by the State Board of Education on December 17, 2010.* Retrieved December 21, 2010, from http://www.fldoe.org/profdev/FEAPSRevisions/

Florida Educator Certification Renewal Requirements (2009). Retrieved April 28, 2010, from http://www.fldoe.org/edcert/renew.asp

Huffman, D., Thomas, K., & Lawrenz, F. (2003). Relationship between professional development, teachers' instructional practices and the achievement of students in science and mathematics. *School Science and Mathematics*, 103(8), 378-87.

Kent, A. (2004). Improving teacher quality through professional development. *Education.* 124(3), 427-35.

U.S. Department of Education. (n.d.). *Family Educational Rights and Privacy Act (FERPA)*. Retrieved April 12, 2010, from http://www.ed.gov/policy/gen/guid/fpco/ferpa/index.html

U. S. Department of Education. (2004, March). *New No Child Left Behind Flexibility: Highly Qualified Teachers.* Retrieved March 28, 2010, from http://www.ed.gov/nclb/methods/teachers/hqtflexibility.html

PROFESSIONAL RESPONSIBILITY AND ETHICAL CONDUCT

Understanding that educators are held to a high moral standard in a community, the effective educator:

- Adheres to the Code of Ethics and the Principles of Professional Conduct of the Education Profession of Florida and fulfills the expected obligations to students, the public and the education profession

Florida Educator Accomplished Practice #6:

PROFESSIONAL RESPONSIBILITY AND ETHICAL CONDUCT

DID YOU KNOW...

Introduction:
In the past few years, the role of the teacher has expanded. In these days of school reform and accountability, it is not enough for the teacher simply to go into the classroom, close the door, and ignore the rest of the school. Today's teachers must demonstrate the highest standards of ethics and principles while meeting the needs of the students, the parents, and members of the community.

Vocabulary:

due process – procedures established to protect the legal rights of individuals; a government agency cannot take adverse action against an individual's Florida Educator certificate or employment contract without adhering to due process procedures

multiple jeopardies – a teacher's inappropriate conduct can result in more than one consequence: termination of employment, criminal penalties, tort liability judgments, fines, and revocation of the Florida Educator Certificate

N.E.A.T. procedure – due process that must be applied by an employing school district when determining an educator does not meet established standards; the district must provide (1) Notice of the specific problem, (2) an Explanation of expectations, (3) Assistance to correct the identified problems, and (4) Time for improvement

property right – a legal entitlement to ownership; for Florida Educators, two examples of property rights are the Florida Educator Certificate and an employment contract

social networking sites – Internet social network services that focus on building online communities of people who share interests and/or activities, or who are interested in exploring the interests and activities of others

standards of proof – the weight of evidence required before a governmental agency can take punitive action against an individual's certificate or contract; the standard is elevated according to the severity of the penalty that may be imposed

Research:

Many professional groups, such as physicians and lawyers, follow a code of ethics that directs the members' conduct. To address the need for common ideals and standards for the teaching profession, the National Education Association (NEA) adopted a Code of Ethics in July 1975.

FLORIDA CODE OF ETHICS AND THE PRINCIPLES OF PROFESSIONAL CONDUCT

Using the Preamble and Principles of the NEA's code as a model, the Florida legislature adopted the Florida Code of Ethics in 1982 and the Principles of Professional Conduct in 1998. These documents identify the standards of conduct expected of Florida educators. The code requires that educators "strive for professional growth" and "exercise the best professional judgment and integrity." It also stresses the educator's obligations to the students, the public, and the teaching profession (Florida Department of Education, 1998).

Below are lists of ethical behaviors expected of Florida teachers, who "by virtue of their leadership capacity" are held to a higher moral standard (Adams v. State of Florida Professional Practices Council, 1981). (See the Appendix for a copy of the Florida Code of Ethics and the Principles of Professional Conduct.)

The Florida teacher's obligations to **students**:
- Maintain respect and confidence of students
- Protect students from conditions harmful to learning
- Protect the health, safety, and emotional well-being of students
- Do not unreasonably deny students access to varying points of view
- Advocate fair and equitable opportunities for all students
- Do not distort subject matter relating to students' academic programs
- Do not intentionally embarrass or disparage students
- Do not violate the legal rights of students
- Never harass or discriminate against students
- Protect students from harassment or discrimination by others
- Maintain confidentiality regarding student records

The Florida teacher's obligations to **parents**:
- Maintain respect and confidence of parents
- Be concerned for the student and the student's potential

The Florida teacher's obligations to the **public**:
- Maintain respect and confidence of members of the community
- Distinguish between personal views of those of the educational institution
- Properly represent facts concerning an educational matter
- Ensure that institutional privileges are not used for personal gain
- Accept no gratuity, gift, or favor that might influence professional judgment
- Offer no gratuity, gift, or favor to obtain advantage

The Florida teacher's obligations to **colleagues**:
- Maintain respect and confidence of colleagues
- Maintain honesty in all professional dealings
- Do not discriminate or harass a professional colleague
- Respect a colleague's exercise of political or civil rights
- Do not make malicious or false statements about a colleague
- Do not coerce or promise special treatment to influence professional decisions of colleagues

The Florida teacher's obligations to **the education profession**:
- Do not misrepresent professional qualifications
- Do not submit false information on any document in connection with professional activities
- Do not make fraudulent statements or fail to disclose important facts on an application for a professional position
- Self-report within 48 hours any arrests or charges involving child abuse and/or the sale/possession of a controlled substance
- Report to appropriate authorities known allegations of a violation of the Florida School Code or Board of Education Rules

WHAT YOU NEED TO KNOW...

Teacher Misconduct

Failure to follow the Code of Ethics and Principles of Professional Conduct may result in suspension, fines, or termination of the educator's certificate. Florida public school districts are required by state statute to investigate alleged misconduct by members of the education profession. If a district's investigation has found that the educator's behavior violated the Code or Principles, the case is referred to the Florida Department of Education's Bureau of Professional Practice Services. This agency administers a state-level grievance process and guarantees that appropriate disciplinary measures are taken against the educator's certificate. Discipline may result in revocation of the teaching certificate, suspension of the certificate, and/or fines. If the educator is found guilty of violating the Code or Principles, the disciplinary action against the educator is posted on the state's Office of Professional Practices' web site for public access.

Inappropriate teacher conduct is reported to law enforcement agencies when criminal acts are committed. Cases are tried in the courts and are not a part of the Florida Department of Education's disciplinary process.

When charges of misconduct are deemed an employment matter, such as incompetence, they are handled by the local school district. According to Florida Statute, teachers who are new to a district are given a "97-day probationary period during which time the employee's contract may be terminated without cause or the employee may resign without breach of contract" (Florida Legislature, 2010, Florida Statute 1012.33(3)(a)4). If an employee has a professional service contract with the school district, the employee is placed on probation and given 90 calendar days, excluding school holidays and vacation periods, to improve. The process school districts use to remediate the educator is referred to as the N.E.A.T. procedure (Florida Department of Education, 2007).

N = NOTICE to the educator that deficiencies exist. Failure to correct the deficiencies may lead to disciplinary action, including termination.

E = Written EXPLANATION of the deficiencies that have been observed by the administrator responsible for the educator's evaluation. The explanation must include suggestions for improvement.

A = ASSISTANCE must be provided to the educator by the administrator. A practical plan for remediating the deficiency must be developed with the input of the educator.

T = Sufficient TIME must be provided for correction of all deficiencies.

Any educator who fails to improve after going through the N.E.A.T. procedure is terminated by the employee's school district.

ETHICAL BEHAVIOR & COMMON SENSE

Educators can avoid ethical and legal complications if they use common sense and professional judgment. Here are some hints that can be valuable (Florida Department of Education, 2007):

Interaction with Students:
- Maintain a professional barrier at all times.
- Never be alone with a student with the doors closed.
- Never flirt or socialize with students.
- Never discuss your personal life with students.
- Never leave your students unsupervised.
- Follow your school district's policies regarding discipline.
- Never harass students or use humorous statements to belittle students.

Record Keeping:
- Adhere to the district's policies regarding purchasing supplies and collecting money.
- Follow the district's grading system.
- Take accurate attendance and maintain lesson plans.
- Communicate with parents and keep copies of the communication.

Reputation in the Community:
- Act and dress professionally.
- Avoid being placed in a position where you will have to defend your actions or behavior.
- Maintain a professional reputation in the school and your community.
- Avoid placing inappropriate information about yourself on the Internet.
- Avoid making disparaging remarks on the social networking sites about coworkers or students.

SUSPENSION & REVOCATION OF CERTIFICATES

Remember, educators are expected to exhibit model behavior both in the school and in the community in which they live. Some of the reasons certificates of Florida educators have been suspended or revoked include (Florida Department of Education, 2007):

- Assault/Battery
- Breach of Contract
- Fraudulent Application for Certificate
- Misappropriation of School Money or Property
- Public Assistance Fraud
- Writing a Worthless Check
- Shoplifting
- Illegal use of Firearm/Weapon
- Incompetence
- Grand Theft/Larceny (includes credit card misuse & possession of stolen property)
- Manslaughter
- Felonies (examples: Arson, Burglary, Counterfeiting, Robbery)
- Misdemeanors (examples: Loitering, Prowling, Trespassing, Violation of Probation)
- Altering Student Grades or Records
- Providing Test Answers to Students
- Giving Alcohol or Other Drugs to Students; Using Alcohol or Drugs with Students
- Absent Without Leave; Falsifying Leave Records
- Sexual Misconduct with Students
- Adult Sexual Misconduct (includes Exposure, Solicitation for Sex, Sexual Harassment of Employees)

WHAT ELSE DO YOU NEED TO KNOW?

Role of Textbooks

The role of classroom textbooks is to organize the basic content for the subject. Although textbooks emphasize important facts and contain activities for learning, teachers must provide and use other resources in the classroom. Remember, all resources must reflect diversity and meet school and district requirements.

Creating a Syllabus

Teachers of grades 7 – 12 might find it helpful to create a syllabus. The syllabus should contain a brief description of the course, a list of materials needed, the course's goals and objectives, types of assignments, grading procedures, and classroom routines and rules.

Extracurricular Activities

Many new teachers are asked by their principals to supervise extracurricular activities, such as becoming club sponsors or athletic coaches. Taking on these roles gives teachers the opportunity to mentor students and interact with their students outside of the classroom. Interaction with students outside of the classroom setting can even lead to increased student achievement.

Before deciding to take on the responsibility of supervising an extracurricular activity, teachers should decide if they have enough time in their daily schedule. Many schools will pay a coach or sponsor a supplement for supervision of an activity.

Fundraising

Teachers who collect money for a fieldtrip or fundraiser should become familiar with the district's policies concerning fundraising. They need to complete the appropriate paperwork and turn in funds in a timely manner. At no time should the teacher ever use the money for anything other than the activity for which it was intended.

School Improvement

Teachers are encouraged to attend or become a member of the School Advisory Council (SAC), a committee consisting of parents, teachers, representatives of local businesses, representatives of the community, and students. This important council reviews the school's state assessment results and creates the school's improvement plan (SIP). The School's Improvement Plan is the document that identifies the school's goals for improving student achievement, as well as the steps needed to meet the identified goals.

Recognizing Student Drug Use/Abuse

Teachers need to recognize the use and abuse of illegal drugs by their students. Some of the most common drugs used are marijuana, Oxycontin, Ecstasy, Adderall, alcohol, and household inhalants (National Institute on Drug Abuse, 2010). When students are suspected of being in the possession of or under the influence of drugs, teachers need to follow district policy.

DRUG	COMMON NAME	APPEARANCE	EFFECTS
Marijuana	grass, pot, weed	Sometimes smoked in water pipe, loosely rolled cigarettes (joints) or hollowed out cigars (blunts)	Users feel happy, giggly and relaxed; can affect coordination, concentration and some memory loss; users often have blood-shot eyes
Oxycontin	Kicker, OC, Oxy, Hillybilly Heroin	Tablets/caplets with "OC" on one side	Users feel euphoric; can cause sweating, vomiting, nausea, and weakness
Ecstasy	MDMA, E, XTC Beans	Tablet form	Users experience an energy high that lasts about 3-6 hours, followed by a slow comedown; sounds, colors, and emotions are more intense; makes individuals more chatty; can cause anxiety, panic attacks, and confusion
Adderall	crosstops, whites, cartwheels	Small round, usually white tablet; prescribed in the treatment of Attention Deficit Hyperactivity Disorder (ADHD)	Users who have not been prescribed the drug may use it to stay awake or as a party drug; can cause dehydration, hot flashes, nausea, and heavy sweating
Alcohol	juice, hooch, red-eye, booze	Liquid; jello shots	Users have mood swings, are less cautious, and often make irresponsible decisions
Household Inhalants	Laughing gas, snappers, poppers, whippets, bold, rush	paint thinner, nail polish remover, contact cement, correction fluid, felt-tip marker fluid, spray paint, hair spray, vegetable oil sprays, whipped cream dispensers	Users sniff items through their nose or mouth, "huffing" (soaking in towels and pressing towels to their mouths), or "bagging" (fumes poured in bags and inhaled); can experience euphoria, dizziness; can cause death or brain damage

Students and Medication

Teachers need to review their district's policy concerning the administration of prescription and over-the-counter medications. In most schools, only a designated individual (nurse or specially trained staff member) can administer medication.

Maintenance of Student Records

Student attendance and grade records, as well as lesson plans, are considered official school documents. Schools are required to maintain these records for auditing purposes.

Using Community Resources

Teachers who have good communication with members of the community can find resources that will enhance their lessons. These resources can include materials for projects, guest speakers, field trip locations, and classroom volunteers.

LET IT SHOW

Below is a list of different methods you can use to demonstrate your accomplishment of **FEAP #6: PROFESSIONAL RESPONSIBILITY AND ETHICAL CONDUCT**.

- ▶ Attend School-Community Meetings: Attend and participate in a Parent-Teacher-Advisory or School Improvement Team meeting.
- ▶ Create a Fundraiser: Create or assist with a fundraiser within the school or community that will help raise money for school equipment or materials.
- ▶ Become a Proctor: Proctor a district or state level assessment test.
- ▶ Become a Mentor: Mentor a student.
- ▶ Create a Syllabus: Create a syllabus for one of your classes.
- ▶ Become a Sponsor or Coach: Volunteer to become a sponsor of a school club or the coach of a sports team.
- ▶ Attend a Child Abuse Recognition Training
- ▶ Attend an Educational Law Class at a University
- ▶ Maintain ethical behavior at all times with students, colleagues, and members of the community.

ACTIVITY OVERVIEW FOR DEMONSTRATING PROFICIENCY IN

FEAP #6: PROFESSIONAL RESPONSIBILITY AND ETHICAL CONDUCT

Activity A: ETHICAL DILEMMAS

Activity B: PUTTING IT ALL TOGETHER

ACTIVITY A

ETHICAL DILEMMAS (FEAP 6)

The purpose of this activity is to provide you with an opportunity to become familiar with the **Code of Ethics** and **Principles of Professional Conduct for the Education Profession in Florida** and then apply these codes to a hypothetical ethical dilemma in written and oral format.

Part 1: Read the **Code of Ethics** and the **Principles of Professional Conduct for the Education Profession in Florida.**

Part 2: Read the ethical dilemmas listed below. Create a written response to each scenario. The response must include your reaction to the situation and citations from the **Code of Ethics** and/or **Principles of Professional Conduct for the Education Profession in Florida** that would support your reaction.

Part 3: Reflection
How will your knowledge about educational law in regards to the **Code of Ethics** and/or **Principles of Professional Conduct for the Education Profession in Florida** impact your teaching? Reflect in depth on your beliefs, assumptions, and classroom practice. Explain how this activity has enabled you to become more informed about ethics and how it has made you more capable as an effective teacher.

Ethical Dilemmas

1. A sixth grade student writes in her journal that her boyfriend has threatened to beat her up if he sees her talking to any boys. When you ask her about the journal entry, she tells you she is scared but that she will "take care of it". How would you handle this situation?

2. One of your students arrives to school 45 minutes late every day. He tells you he is late because he has to care for his baby sister until his mother comes home from her night job. He is a good student and always makes up the work he has missed. Should you intervene?

3. Four teachers are sitting in the stands watching a football game. Sitting behind them, you overhear the teachers discussing students by name. Parents and students sitting next to the teachers can also overhear their conversation. Should you do or say something to the teachers?

4. All the students in your class are required to write a poem for the Renaissance Fair. One of the student's poems is of very high quality and does not represent the work he has done in the past. You suspect his parents helped him write the poem. How do you handle this situation?

5. A student writes in her journal that she is overweight, has no friends, and no one would miss her if she died. What should you do?

6. You have just found out that you can make some money by tutoring one of your students during your off hours. The parents will even pay you extra money if you can provide transportation for their child. For convenience, you drive the student to your apartment after school, tutor the student, and then drive the student home. Is this okay to do? Why or why not?

7. The teachers in your school have received training on how to administer the state assessment. You and another teacher have been assigned to the same classroom. You notice the other teacher is making comments to the students saying, "You might want to look again at Number Six," or, "You really should look over that page again." Should you say or do anything?

ACTIVITY B

PUTTING IT ALL TOGETHER (FEAP 6)

Directions: Review the following scenarios. What would you do? Which Florida Educator Accomplished Practice helped you make your decision?

1. One of your students is a loner in class—she does not interact with other students. She seems unhappy all the time and you are concerned. How can you help her?

2. You notice your students are apathetic during class. They seldom comment and then only in response to your questions. What can you do?

3. One of your students is verbally aggressive towards other students in class. He calls them names, brags about beating up other students, and is creating an atmosphere of hostility. What will you do?

4. Two LEP students in your class have trouble completing the assignments. Provide suggestions for solving this problem.

5. One of your students seldom completes the assignments and homework. When you speak with him, he tells you that it does not make any difference if he completes the work because he will fail anyway. What can you do?

6. You have received the previous year's state assessment scores for your students. How will you use this data?

7. You have four students who run into your class every day to avoid being tardy. This behavior has become disruptive and dangerous. How can you eliminate this problem?

8. You are required to enter grades in the computer. You are not familiar with the software program. What will you do?

9. Your students are seating themselves according to racial groups. There is no interaction among the groups. How can you fix this problem?

10. You are having problems with classroom management. The students are out of control. What can you do?

11. One of your colleagues tells you she needs to withdraw some money from her bank. However, she has an appointment after school and the bank will be closed by the time she gets there. She asks if you will "lend" her $20 from the fieldtrip money you collected today. She promises to pay you back tomorrow. What will you do?

12. One of your assignments requires your students to do research on the Internet; however, the computer lab is being re-wired. A quick survey of your class indicates that all but one of your students has access to the Internet in their homes. What are you going to do?

13. You have a gifted student who is failing your class. What can you do?

14. Your students earned grades of "C" or lower on the last test. What should you do?

RESOURCES

Adams v. State of Florida Professional Practices Council, 406 So 2nd 1170 Fla. 1st DCA, 1981.

Code of Ethics of the Education Profession, National Education Association. Retrieved April 28, 2010, from http://www.nea.org/aboutnea/code.html

Florida Department of Education. (1998). *Code of Ethics – Education Profession.* Retrieved May 10, 2010, from http://www.fldoe.org/edstandards/code_of_ethics.asp

Florida Department of Education (2007). *Professionalism through integrity: The Code of Ethics and the Principles of Professional Conduct.* Retrieved August 10, 2010, from http://www.fldoe.org/dpe/publications/coe-training.pdf

Florida Department of Education. (2010). *6A-5.065-The Educator Accomplished Practices as approved by the State Board of Education on December 17, 2010.* Retrieved December 21, 2010, from http://www.fldoe.org/profdev/FEAPSRevisions/

Florida Legislature. (2010). *The 2010 Florida Statutes: Chapter 1012.33—Contracts with instructional staff, supervisors, and school principals.* Retrieved August 29, 2010, from http://www.leg.state.fl.us/statutes/index.cfm?App_mode=Display_Statute&Search_String=&URL=1000-1099/1012/Sections/1012.33.html

National Institute on Drug Abuse. (2010). *Drugs of Abuse Information.* Retrieved May 12, 2010, from http://www.drugabuse.gov/drugpages/

TeenDrugAbuse.US. *Teenage abuse of common household products.* Retrieved May 12, 2010, from http://www.teendrugabuse.us/household_products.html

UCSB Alcohol & Drug Program. *Info on alcohol & drugs.* Retrieved May 12, 2010, from http://alcohol.sa.ucsb.edu/Students/InfoAlcoholnDrug/index.aspx

APPENDIX

- Florida Code of Ethics
- Florida Principles of Professional Conduct
- The Interstate Teacher Assessment and Support Consortium (InTASC) Standards and Relationship to the Florida Educator Accomplished Practices

Code of Ethics of the Education Profession
6B-1.001 Code of Ethics of the Education Profession in Florida.

1. *The educator values the worth and dignity of every person, the pursuit of truth, devotion to excellence, acquisition of knowledge, and the nurture of democratic citizenship. Essential to the achievement of these standards are the freedom to learn and to teach and the guarantee of equal opportunity for all.*
2. *The educator's primary professional concern will always be for the student and for the development of the student's potential. The educator will therefore strive for professional growth and will seek to exercise the best professional judgment and integrity.*
3. *Aware of the importance of maintaining the respect and confidence of one's colleagues, of students, of parents, and of other members of the community, the educator strives to achieve and sustain the highest degree of ethical conduct.*

Specific Authority 229.053(1), 231.546(2)(b) FS. Law Implemented 231.546(2)(b) FS. History - New 3-24-65, Amended 8-9-69, Repromulgated 12-5-74, Amended 8-12-81, 7-6-82, Formerly 6B-1.01.

Source: Florida Department of Education (2007) Professionalism through integrity: The Code of Ethics and the Principles of Professional Conduct.

Principles of Professional Conduct of the Education Profession
6B-1.006 Principles of Professional Conduct for the Education Profession in Florida.

1. The following disciplinary rule shall constitute the Principles of Professional Conduct for the Education Profession in Florida.
2. Violation of any of these principles shall subject the individual to revocation or suspension of the individual educator's certificate, or the other penalties as provided by law
3. Obligation to the student requires that the individual:
   a. Shall make reasonable effort to protect the student from conditions harmful to learning and/or to the student's mental and/or physical health and/or safety.
   b. Shall not unreasonably restrain a student from independent action in pursuit of learning.
   c. Shall not unreasonably deny a student access to diverse points of view.
   d. Shall not intentionally suppress or distort subject matter relevant to a student's academic program.
   e. Shall not intentionally expose a student to unnecessary embarrassment or disparagement.
   f. Shall not intentionally violate or deny a student's legal rights.
   g. Shall not harass or discriminate against any student on the basis of race, color, religion, sex, age, national or ethnic origin, political beliefs, marital status, handicapping condition, sexual orientation, or social and family background and shall make reasonable effort to assure that each student is protected from harassment or discrimination.
   h. Shall not exploit a relationship with a student for personal gain or advantage.
   i. Shall keep in confidence personally identifiable information obtained in the course of professional service, unless disclosure serves professional purposes or is required by law.
4. Obligation to the public requires that the individual:
   a. Shall take reasonable precautions to distinguish between personal views and those of any educational institution or organization with which the individual is affiliated.
   b. Shall not intentionally distort or misrepresent facts concerning an educational matter in direct or indirect public expression.
   c. Shall not use institutional privileges for personal gain or advantage.
   d. Shall accept no gratuity, gift, or favor that might influence professional judgment.
   e. Shall offer no gratuity, gift, or favor to obtain special advantages.
5. Obligation to the profession of education requires that the individual:
   a. Shall maintain honesty in all professional dealings.
   b. Shall not on the basis of race, color, religion, sex, age, national or ethnic origin, political beliefs, marital status, handicapping condition if otherwise qualified, or social and family background deny to a colleague professional benefits or advantages or participation in any professional organization.

c. Shall not interfere with a colleague's exercise of political or civil rights and responsibilities.

d. Shall not engage in harassment or discriminatory conduct which unreasonably interferes with an individual's performance of professional or work responsibilities or with the orderly processes of education or which creates a hostile, intimidating, abusive, offensive, or oppressive environment; and, further, shall make reasonable effort to assure that each individual is protected from such harassment or discrimination.

e. Shall not make malicious or intentionally false statements about a colleague.

f. Shall not use coercive means or promise special treatment to influence professional judgments of colleagues.

g. Shall not misrepresent one's own professional qualifications.

h. Shall not submit fraudulent information on any document in connection with professional activities.

i. Shall not make any fraudulent statement or fail to disclose a material fact in one's own or another's application for a professional position.

j. Shall not withhold information regarding a position from an applicant or misrepresent an assignment or conditions of employment.

k. Shall provide upon the request of the certificated individual a written statement of specific reason for recommendations that lead to the denial of increments, significant changes in employment, or termination of employment.

l. Shall not assist entry into or continuance in the profession of any person known to be unqualified in accordance with these Principles of Professional Conduct for the Education Profession in Florida and other applicable Florida Statutes and State Board of Education Rules.

m. Shall self-report within forty-eight (48) hours to appropriate authorities (as determined by district) any arrests/charges involving the abuse of a child or the sale and/or possession of a controlled substance. Such notice shall not be considered an admission of guilt nor shall such notice be admissible for any purpose in any proceeding, civil or criminal, administrative or judicial, investigatory or adjudicatory. In addition, shall self-report any conviction, finding of guilt, withholding of adjudication, commitment to a pretrial diversion program, or entering of a plea of guilty or Nolo Contendre for any criminal offense other than a minor traffic violation within forty-eight (48) hours after the final judgment. When handling sealed and expunged records disclosed under this rule, school districts shall comply with the confidentiality provisions of Sections 943.0585(4)(c) and 943.059(4)(c), Florida Statutes.

n. Shall report to appropriate authorities any known allegation of a violation of the Florida School Code or State Board of Education Rules as defined in Section 1012.795(1), Florida Statutes.

o. Shall seek no reprisal against any individual who has reported any allegation of a violation of the Florida School Code or State Board of Education Rules as defined in Section1012.795(1), Florida Statutes.

p. Shall comply with the conditions of an order of the Education Practices Commission.

q. Shall, as the supervising administrator, cooperate with the Education Practices Commission in monitoring the probation of a subordinate.

Specific Authority 229.053(1), 231.546(2)(b) FS. Law Implemented 231.546(2), 231.28 FS. History New 7-6-82, Amended 12-20-83, Formerly 6B-1.06, Amended 8-10-92, 12-29-98.

Source: Florida Department of Education (2007) Professionalism through integrity: The Code of Ethics and the Principles of Professional Conduct.

MY RECORD

DEMONSTRATION OF THE
FLORIDA EDUCATOR ACCOMPLISHED PRACTICES (FEAP)

Directions: Use the following pages to record your demonstration of each of the Florida Educator Accomplished Practices. Place a ✔ in the appropriate box, using the key below. An example is provided on this page.

KEY: LS = Demonstration from "Let It Show" section of *Resource Guide*

     A = Demonstration from "Activity" section of *Resource Guide*

     O = Other (Identify)

LS	A	O	*(a) Aligns instruction with state-adopted standards at the appropriate level of rigor*
	✔		Demonstration: *Using Activity A, I created a lesson plan on _____ and identified the Sunshine State State Standard for the lesson.* Date Demonstrated: *January 30, 2011*
LS	**A**	**O**	*(b) Sequences lessons and concepts to ensure coherence and required prior knowledge*
✔			Demonstration: *I created a three-day unit on _____. The lessons were sequential and I ensured my students had the required prior knowledge before moving on to the next lesson.* Date Demonstrated: *March 12, 2011*

MY RECORD

DEMONSTRATION OF THE
FLORIDA EDUCATOR ACCOMPLISHED PRACTICES (FEAP)

Name: _____

Directions: Use the following pages to record your demonstration of each of the Florida Educator Accomplished Practices. Place a ✔ in the appropriate box, using the key below. An example is provided on this page.

KEY: LS = Demonstration from "Let It Show" section of *Resource Guide*
      A = Demonstration from "Activity" section of *Resource Guide*
      O = Other (Identify)

FEAP #1: INSTRUCTIONAL DESIGN AND LESSON PLANNING

LS	A	O	*(a) Aligns instruction with state-adopted standards at the appropriate level of rigor*
			Demonstration: Date Demonstrated:
LS	**A**	**O**	*(b) Sequences lessons and concepts to ensure coherence and required prior knowledge*
			Demonstration: Date Demonstrated:
LS	**A**	**O**	*(c) Designs instruction for students to achieve mastery*
			Demonstration: Date Demonstrated:

LS	A	O	(d) *Selects appropriate formative assessments to monitor learning*
			Demonstration: Date Demonstrated:
LS	A	O	(e) *Uses a variety of data, independently, and in collaboration with colleagues to evaluate learning outcomes, adjust planning and continuously improve the effectiveness of the lessons*
			Demonstration: Date Demonstrated:
LS	A	O	(f) *Develops learning experiences that require students to demonstrate a variety of applicable skills and competencies*
			Demonstration: Date Demonstrated:

FEAP #2: THE LEARNING ENVIRONMENT

LS	A	O	(a) *Organizes, allocates, and manages the resources of time, space, and attention*
			Demonstration: Date Demonstrated:
LS	A	O	(b) *Manages individual and class behaviors through a well-planned management system*
			Demonstration: Date Demonstrated:
LS	A	O	(c) *Conveys high expectations to all students*
			Demonstration: Date Demonstrated:
LS	A	O	(d) *Respects students' cultural, linguistic and family background*
			Demonstration: Date Demonstrated:

LS	A	O	(e) Models clear, acceptable oral and written communication skills
			Demonstration: Date Demonstrated:
LS	A	O	(f) Maintains a climate of openness, inquiry, fairness and support
			Demonstration: Date Demonstrated:
LS	A	O	(g) Integrates current information and communication technologies
			Demonstration: Date Demonstrated:
LS	A	O	(h) Adapts the learning environment to accommodate the differing needs and diversity of students
			Demonstration: Date Demonstrated:
LS	A	O	(i) Utilizes current and emerging assistive technologies that enable students to participate in high-quality communication interactions and achieve their educational goals
			Demonstration: Date Demonstrated:

FEAP #3: INSTRUCTIONAL DELIVERY AND FACILITATION

LS	A	O	
LS	**A**	**O**	*(a) Deliver engaging and challenging lessons*
			Demonstration: Date Demonstrated:
LS	**A**	**O**	*(b) Deepen and enrich students' understanding through content area literacy strategies, verbalization of thought, and application of the subject matter*
			Demonstration: Date Demonstrated:
LS	**A**	**O**	*(c) Identify gaps in students' subject matter knowledge*
			Demonstration: Date Demonstrated:
LS	**A**	**O**	*(d) Modify instruction to respond to preconceptions or misconceptions*
			Demonstration: Date Demonstrated:
LS	**A**	**O**	*(e) Relate and integrate the subject matter with other disciplines and life experiences*
			Demonstration: Date Demonstrated:

LS	A	O	(f) Employ higher-order questioning techniques
			Demonstration: Date Demonstrated:
LS	A	O	(g) Apply varied instructional strategies and resources, including appropriate technology, to provide comprehensive instruction, and to teach for student understanding
			Demonstration: Date Demonstrated:
LS	A	O	(h) Differentiate instruction based on an assessment of student learning needs and recognition of individual differences in students
			Demonstration: Date Demonstrated:
LS	A	O	(i) Support, encourage, and provide immediate and specific feedback to students to promote student achievement
			Demonstration: Date Demonstrated:
LS	A	O	(j) Utilize student feedback to monitor instructional needs and to adjust instruction
			Demonstration: Date Demonstrated:

FEAP #4: ASSESSMENT

LS	A	O	
LS	**A**	**O**	*(a) Analyzes and applies data from multiple assessments and measures to diagnose students' learning needs, informs instructions based on those needs, and drives the learning process*
			Demonstration: Date Demonstrated:
LS	**A**	**O**	*(b) Designs and aligns formative and summative assessments that match learning objectives and lead to mastery*
			Demonstration: Date Demonstrated:
LS	**A**	**O**	*(c) Uses a variety of assessment tools to monitor student progress, achievement and learning gains*
			Demonstration: Date Demonstrated:
LS	**A**	**O**	*(d) Modifies assessments and testing conditions to accommodate learning styles and varying levels of knowledge*
			Demonstration: Date Demonstrated:

LS	A	O	(e) Shares the importance and outcomes of student assessment data with the student and the student's parent/caregiver
			Demonstration:
			Date Demonstrated:
LS	A	O	(f) Applies technology to organize and integrate assessment information
			Demonstration:
			Date Demonstrated:

FEAP #5: CONTINUOUS IMPROVEMENT

LS	A	O	*(a)* *Designs purposeful professional goals to strengthen the effectiveness of instruction based on students' needs*
			Demonstration: Date Demonstrated:
LS	A	O	*(b)* *Examines and uses data-informed research to improve instruction and student achievement*
			Demonstration: Date Demonstrated:
LS	A	O	*(c)* *Collaborates with the home, school and larger communities to foster communication and to support student learning and continuous improvement*
			Demonstration: Date Demonstrated:
LS	A	O	*(d)* *Engages in targeted professional growth opportunities and reflective practices*
			Demonstration: Date Demonstrated:

LS	A	O	(e) *Implements knowledge and skills learned in professional development in the teaching and learning process*
			Demonstration: Date Demonstrated:

FEAP #6: PROFESSIONAL RESPONSIBILITY AND ETHICAL CONDUCT

LS	A	O	*Adheres to the Code of Ethics and the Principles of Professional Conduct of the Education Profession of Florida, pursuant to State Board of Education Rules 6B-1.001 and 6B1.006, F.A.C. and fulfills the expected obligations to the students, the public and the education profession*
			Demonstration: Date Demonstrated:

INDEX